For Enda.
An ethical Offering.
With love & admiration,

Gail.

The Curious Case

of Inequality

Creator: Freyne, Gail Grossman, author.

Title: The curious case of inequality : a journey for justice with Dorothy L Sayers / Gail Grossman Freyne.

ISBN: 9781925486810 (paperback)
        9781925486827 (hardback)
        9781925486834 (ebook : ePub)
        9781925486841 (ebook : Kindle)
        9781925486858 (ebook : PDF)

Notes: Includes bibliographical references and index.

Subjects: Sayers, Dorothy L. (Dorothy Leigh), 1893-1957.
Ecofeminism.
Ecotheology.

Cover design and Layout by Astrid Sengkey

Text: Minion Pro size 10 &11

Published by:

An imprint of the ATF Press Publishing Group owned by ATF (Australia) Ltd.
PO Box 504
Hindmarsh, SA 5007
ABN 90 116 359 963
www.atfpress.com
Making a lasting impact

The Curious Case of Inequality

A Journey for Justice with Dorothy L Sayers

Gail Grossman Freyne

ATF Theology
Adelaide
2017

IN HONOUR OF TWO REMARKABLE WOMEN

BRIDGET AND SARAH

Table of Contents

Acknowledgements

I find it hard these days to think of Dorothy Sayers without thinking of Joan O'Farrell Fitzgerald (1923-1999), political and cultural adviser to her husband and former Taoiseach, Garret Fitzgerald. When the talk of politics and theology was becoming repetitive, we would ease our chairs back from the dinner table, acknowledge that we both had a hopelessly romantic streak and talk about Peter Wimsey and Harriet Vane. I will always be grateful to her for those conversations that came with a twinkle.

For the other repetitive work that ensured that I was not being repetitive, I am again grateful to the careful reading—twice—of this manuscript by my dear friend and taskmaster, Joan D Chittister. Most of what I have thought would never have found its way into print had it not been for her persistent urging and constant encouragement. I am equally grateful to Angela M Arthur for the painstaking work of producing the final edit.

For the literally life-changing event of learning to analyse the fact of sex and the concept of gender, I am always indebted to Katherine Zappone, TD, Minister for Children and Youth Affairs in the current Irish government, to Ailbhe Smyth, co-founder and Director of the Women's Education, Research & Resource Centre at University College Dublin from 1990-2006 and to Anne Fogarty, Professor of English, University College Dublin who was such a patient guide to my first literary effort.

I am also grateful to all my friends who constantly require accountability, insisting on the reasons on which I base my assertions.

If they read this book they will no doubt recognise themselves on many of its pages.

I would also like to thank Professor Elaine Wainwright, who provided the happy suggestion of sending this manuscript to ATF Press, which with the help of my publisher, Hilary D Regan, became a book.

Preface

On 26 July 1926 in the *Yorkshire Post*, the novelist, journalist, campaigner and feminist, Winifred Holtby, wrote: 'I dislike everything that feminism implies . . . I want to be about the work in which my real interests lie, the study of inter-race relationships, the writing of novels and so forth. But while the inequality exists, while injustice is done and opportunity denied to the great majority of women, I shall have to be a feminist.' Holtby's sense of exasperation that even after the vote had been won, many battles remained to be fought around women's equality, and her feeling that all she wanted was to take her rightful place as an equal member of society without having constantly to defend that place, was shared by other women writers of the time, not least by Dorothy L Sayers. Despite her many notable achievements as theologian, novelist, poet, playwright and translator, Dorothy L Sayers (1893-1957) remained ambivalent about feminism, as Virginia Woolf, for example, was not, and for similar reasons to Holtby: Sayers was impatient for the whole feminist debate to be concluded so that women could take their place alongside men as equal human beings.

Yet, as Virginia Woolf knew and Gail Freyne argues in this book, the feminist phase cannot be so easily skipped over in favour of some illusory postfeminist equality. In her essays, *A Room of One's Own* (1929) and *Three Guineas* (1938), Woolf argued that asserting women's right to equal treatment involved not only implementing certain laws and educational reforms but changing an entire culture's mindset about the relationship between women and men. Women would have to cease acting as 'looking-glasses possessing the magic and delicious power of reflecting the figure of man at twice its natural size' while men would have to stop clinging to 'unmitigated masculinity' and become 'woman-manly or man-womanly'. Woolf gives examples of writers like Shakespeare, Coleridge and Keats who, she claims, achieved greatness through their ability to access both genders. Or, as Gail Freyne puts it in chapter 2, they were men who had learned to 'think with their feelings'.

In the 1930s Dorothy L Sayers published three detective novels —*Strong Poison* (1930), *Have His Carcase* (1932) and *Gaudy Night* (1936)—that in the course of delineating the developing relationship between Harriet Vane and Lord Peter Wimsey, make some prescient observations about the unequal relationship between the sexes. In these novels Harriet remarks on, among other things, the reservation of certain jobs for men, society's assumption that women are natural care-givers, the double standards around sexual behaviour, the loss of identity for women on marriage, women's failure to take responsibility for their own lives, obstacles in the workplace for women who are mothers, the need for financial independence. Many of these observations unfortunately and unbelievably, given the nearly eighty odd years that have lapsed since Sayers wrote them, still hold good for today.

In using Sayers's novels as a base and drawing on her own years of experience as a psychotherapist, Freyne makes some important points about the still unequal relationship between the sexes and the difficulty of addressing those issues in a postfeminist culture that assumes women have already achieved equality. There are chapters on women's work in the home, domestic violence, the lack of women in top management posts and in political life, cultural pressures around marriage and body image, and sexual harassment. Freyne offers some solutions too—but for these you will have to read her stimulating and thought-provoking book.

Professor Heather Ingman,
Trinity College,
Dublin.

Introduction

Detective novel or philosophical treatise? When it comes to the creation of those delightful offsprings of the mind of Dorothy L Sayers (1893–1957), Lord Peter Wimsey and Ms Harriet Vane, the answer is both. Three of her novels, *Strong Poison*, *Have His Carcase*, and *Gaudy Night*, written between 1930 and 1936, are set within the context of their developing relationship.[1] Love at first sight for one, doubt and soul-searching in the other; the pursuer and the pursued. This burgeoning love affair provides Sayers with the perfect vehicle to air her views about women and men and their relationships. While these books are always fun and engaging—which alone would render them worthwhile—they are also cunningly crafted works that illuminate the shocking fact that the problems that faced couples in the 1930s are all too similar to the ones that continue to worry relationships to this day. Equality between the sexes is still the chimera that it was before the second World War—tantalizingly close but still just beyond our reach. If you don't believe me then take a trip with myself and Dorothy L Sayers, the creator of the aristocratic sleuth, Lord Peter Wimsey, and his beloved, that independent writer of detective fiction, Harriet Vane.

Unfortunately, although these characters were as witty, quirky, independent and downright combative as Sayers herself, she tired of them when her readers were still begging for more. One of her biographers, Barbara Reynolds, who was also a close friend, offers one explanation as to why Sayers moved to different literary genres:

---

1. References throughout to these three novels are taken from the New English Library edition published in London in 2003.

'She had come to the conclusion that detective stories tended to have a bad effect on people, making them believe that there was one neat solution for all human ills, and she would have no more part in encouraging such an attitude'.[2] But maybe, as Carolyn Heilbrun suggests, this was mere 'folderol', to mask the fact that while having created such an independent woman in Harriet Vane was unusual, to sustain her in the England of the 30s would have required a miracle. Harriet's story ends in the traditional way, with marriage to Peter and subsequent motherhood while Peter continued to 'quest' in detection and diplomacy.[3]

Nonetheless, it is possible that Sayers felt that feminist theory and practice also had a bad effect on people and for the same reason. She was frequently at pains during her lifetime to disassociate herself from this movement. In her monograph, 'Are Women Human?',[4] she makes this explicit, telling us that she does not want to be defined as a modern feminist because she sees it as a movement that often does more harm than good. Her line of thinking is that feminists make a mistake when, as she sees it, they play identity politics. They do this when they talk about women's rights instead of focusing on human rights. Yet even as Sayers talks of feminism as if it was unitary, cohesive and having no internal tensions or contradictions, she becomes angry when women are themselves homogenized and treated as if they were all the same. When she was asked what was women's point of view on issue X, she suggests that we ask a particular woman her view. She sarcastically reminds us that nobody asks what is mens' point of view on issue X. Yet, still, today, political pundits are fond of burbling on about how important it is to capture the 'women's vote' but with nary a reference to any 'men's vote'.

For Sayers, men and women are all human beings and entitled to the same rights and privileges. This makes her, and anyone who holds the same view, a feminist. Anyone who does not hold this view is sexist. She asserted it in the 1930s and many of us advocate this view today yet it does not make it so. In admitting that she had what

---

2. Barbara Reynolds, *A Mind in Love: Dorothy L Sayers, Her Life and Soul*, (New York: St Martin's Press, 1993).
3. Carolyn Heilbrun, *Writing a Woman's Life* (New York: Ballantine Books, 1988), 58.
4. Dorothy L Sayers, *Are Women Human* (Grand Rapids: Eerdmans, 2005).

she described as a foolish complex against allying herself publicly with anything labeled feminist, Sayers was expressing a still constant anxiety of today's women. Like many women today, I am sure she would gladly have allied herself publicly with any movement that sought to end racism. Likewise, most of us feel free to rage against discrimination made on the basis of social or economic class, or sexual orientation, or age, or even the treatment of other animals. Working to put an end to all forms of discrimination is considered to be an admirable occupation. Yet, when you get angry about sexism, you run into everything from irritation to panicked vilification.

How is it that there are still some people who assume that the search for equality between men and women is either an anachronism or morphs into a hatred of men?

It is a fear of change that causes the ongoing backlash against feminist values and ideals. It is this backlash that is the cause of my impatience. By far and away the most successful strategy of the anti-feminist has been to declare that we now inhabit a post-feminist world. It is a static story, one that tells us that all the goals have been achieved, women can now do whatever they want without having to fight any form of discrimination. How often have you heard this? There is no glass ceiling, well women might still be only branch managers but they will be regional managers very soon now. The new man is really into co-parenting and before you can say pass the Johnson's baby powder, he will be sharing the housework.

The corollary to this strategy of the backlash is that because we are, it is asserted, in a post-feminist world—there is no longer any cause to talk about feminism. The feminist cause is, in fact, *passé*. At best, feminism is a boring anachronism; at worst, it is the F word. And if you want to talk about it you will not find yourself in the midst of comforting numbers, not solidly mainstream. You are not acting in the best interests of society; you are an annoyance, an irritation, and definitely a threat to the family. You might be called strident, or, worst of all, just plain yawning, boring. You are none of these things if you talk about racism, which we all know still exists. Feminism, the movement that addresses the entire human race, as it seeks equality between the two halves of humanity, is the one, major area of discrimination that still, today, many women fear to talk about because many men do not want to hear about it.

We need a little reality check here: while we share a common humanity there are important and meaningful differences between all of us. In every case, difference means not better than or less than, simply different. Some differences we have been born with; they are part of our biology. Men tend to be taller and stronger. Men have square knees and women have round ones. Chapter 9 deals with violence against women and Chapter 7 with the problems associated with the shape of women's bodies.

There are other differences too, ones that we have learned. In the years of being confined to the home and excluded from public life, women have become experts at relationships and in the practice of the virtue of care. Chapter 5 discusses how this virtue has been aligned with women while men governed states and churches and armies but looked to the concepts of rights and justice to order human institutions and societies. Chapter 3 describes the bifurcation of reason and emotion and the problems that arise when he thinks and decides, she feels and demurs. We call these different ways of behaving gender stereotypes. Chapters 1, 19 and 20 that define gender, feminism and friendship respectively, deal with problems and solutions when we turn the spotlight on women's place in the home and the workplace, as mothers and entrepreneurs and politicians. Chapters 16 and 17 discuss money and power and explain why there are still more suits on every page of the newspaper, on boards of major companies and on benches of parliamentarians and bishops.

A mature feminism, one that informs the inclusive brand of psychotherapy with which I engage, has never asked for more than half. It knows precisely what Sayers never understood that it knew: that women and men are both mind and body, equally rational and equally emotional. To me, this is a truth so manifest that I feel ready to buy billboard space to ask, 'what is it about this picture that you don't get?' What causes my impatience is that, as I sit on my verandah, quietly rocking in the evening sun, looking back over my life to date as girl child, daughter, lawyer, wife, mother, psychotherapist, grandmother . . . I see the thousands of books that have been written on the subject of feminism, I acknowledge my own tiny contribution, and I wonder, yet again, why is the message not getting through.

The intervening period of eighty years, between the publication of Sayers' detective stories and today represents, actuarially speaking, in this part of the world, about the lifetime of one woman. In the course of this journey with Harriet and Peter, we will see what Sayers had to say about the place of women in society. It will become apparent how many of our attitudes and how much of our belief systems have changed, and how little. When we discover that much of women's lives are still governed by the morals and the mores of the 1930s, why, you too might even become impatient. You might even find it shocking that as we race through the second decade of the new millennium, I am agreeing with everything a woman had to say on the condition of women in the 1930s.

Yet, change is in the air and when change is in the air, change happens. Even as we take a clear look with Sayers at where we have been, it becomes easier for us to see where we might go. Rather than sit back and wait for the revolution, I am urging that each of us engages with new forms of behaviour and new sets of ideas that will bring us to a genuine, a fully inclusive post-feminist world where equality between men and women is not something to which we pay lip service, is not a mere aspiration, but the defining characteristic of our daily, human lives. As Wimsey might say, 'That would be rather jolly!'

Eilund sniffed scornfully, and departed to fill the kettle at a tap on the landing . . . 'No thanks'—as Wimsey advanced to carry the kettle— 'I'm quite capable of carrying six pints of water'.

'Crushed again!' said Wimsey.

'Eilund disapproves of conventional courtesies between the sexes,' said Marjorie.

'Very well,' replied Wimsey amiably, 'I will adopt an attitude of passive decoration.'

Strong Poison

Chapter 1
Gender: Are you Being Served?

The 'conventional courtesies between the sexes', harmless enough in themselves, mask a dance of complementarity between men and women that is the essence of strong poison.

Opening doors, pulling out chairs and walking on the outside of the footpath on a rainy day all look harmless enough, but why did these practices originate? What motivated them? Do these quaint little customs tell us anything about the essence of 'maleness' and 'femaleness'? Or, do they really speak to us about the ways in which we have socially constructed the apparently harmless, but actually very fraught, categories of 'masculinity' and 'femininity'? Which sex benefits from these practices; is it women who are really being served?

To answer these questions, we first need to answer a more foundational one: Is there a difference between sex and gender? And, if so, exactly what is this difference? The term gender is often used to denote one sex or another, and given the context, we nearly always know what is meant. For example, when filling out a form, we are often asked what is our gender, when the information that is really sought is to which sex do we belong. In our day to day conversations this slippage between the two terms causes no confusion. However, when we come to less concrete areas of our lives, our philosophical musings on what does it mean to be a 'man' or a 'woman', we need to define sex and gender more precisely. Without clarity on these terms all our discussions about men and women become so hopelessly tangled that they are either useless or dangerous. The confusion that ensues leads to feminists being misunderstood and misrepresented.

When used as a mere description of our sexual differences the term gender is not judgmental. But if, for example, sex is collapsed into gender then ensuing interpretations become judgmental: All men (sex) are seen to be as problematic as the patriarchal construction of society (gender). The most successful move of the anti-feminist is to conflate the two categories which enables them, by this wicked sleight of hand, to accuse all feminists of being men-haters. The same manoeuver also makes other women fearful of publically joining the vilified group even when they are in private agreement. No woman, happily single and loving her dad or happily married and loving her son wants to be labeled what she knows she is not—a man-hater.

One way to achieve clarity is to use the term 'sex' to denote our biology, to refer to the natural, reproductive bodies of the female and the male. 'Gender', on the other hand, becomes a cultural term, something we have invented. It is the social description of our sexual differences. We use it to describe the characteristics which we have overlaid onto the natural equality of the maleness and femaleness with which we were born. It is this overlaying process which socially constructs what we call our 'masculine' and 'feminine' identities. So, we start out equal but then we are taught to behave in ways that are characteristically masculine or feminine, and it is these behaviours that disrupt our natural equality. We are taught that men are rational and clear thinking, and that little boys shouldn't cry. It is women who are emotional and intuitive, and they have permission to cry at birth, deaths and marriages and every life event in between. Once we have learned our 'boy' and 'girl' lessons, we are left in no doubt as to which set of characteristics are the most highly valued: we esteem the clarity and calmness of male reason and denigrate the chaos and agitation female emotion.

Furthermore, we imbibe that poisonous brew that tells us that certain behaviours are appropriate for only one sex and must not be practiced by the other: women should never demonstrate masculine characteristics nor men feminine ones.

In so many ways, gender is dangerous. Because it is a definition of what it means to be masculine or feminine it outlines the behaviour expected of each sex. Because a man cannot afford to be, or even to be thought of, as feminine, the corollary is that he is always being nudged towards the outer limits of his masculine identity. So, boys and men drink too much and drive too fast. They kill themselves at speed in far greater numbers than do women all for the sake of being masculine. Men work crazy hours, striving to be wealthy and successful. They make themselves ill, even unto death, with stress induced heart attacks. Insurance companies recognise these facts. In the same way, the good woman bears no masculine characteristics. Girls and women wear heels that ruin their feet and backs and they are still dieting when they are eighty. Advertising agencies recognise these facts. She attends to her body and he attends to his bank balance. She loses her sense of herself to the degree that she defers to him; he loses his sense of himself by thinking he is better than he is. He is burdened by too much responsibility in the public world, she by too much responsibility in the private one. Both of them lose out on the benefits enjoyed by the other in the worlds they are not supposed to inhabit.

Gender is dangerous because it takes all of human potential and divides it by two. Gender takes all human attributes and virtues and allocates half to one sex and half to the other. By the very act of splitting human potential we make it impossible to conceive of what it might mean for any one person to be *fully* human, the very fact that Sayers thought was self-evident. Real, masculine men are rational, assertive, decisive, independent and the ones who are presumed to be capable of 'carrying six pints of water'. These attributes are all very fine but represent at most half of human potential. Real, feminine women are intuitive, emotional, nurturing, dependent and always 'to adopt an air of passive decoration'. Again, only half of what they could be.

It is this radical separation of men and women into two camps, each partitioned from the other by rigid rules of social behaviour, that has not only initiated 'The War of the Sexes' but continues to perpetuate the misery. By means of this patriarchal philosophy that we call gender, men and women are actually constructed in opposition to each other. Feminism is the philosophy that recognises that the sexes were born equal to each other. Testosterone does not mean that men are condemned to violence. Estrogen does not mean that women are born better carers. It is feminism that asserts that all human virtues are inherent in every person. It is feminism that is suing for harmony between the sexes.

But all this divisiveness is a thing of the past, right? We are no longer split into two warring yet supposedly complementary camps. We know that women who design cities are just as rational as men, and men who change nappies can be equally as caring as women. Even in 1930, Sayers knew that we had to make all human virtues and attributes available to both sexes so that each of us could be a full and complete human being. She speaks to us through the medium of a letter, sent by Miss Kitty Climpson who is off doing a bit of detecting at the behest of her employer, Lord Peter Wimsey:

> I had **no** difficulty in getting a room at the Station Hotel,
> **late** as it was. In the old days, an **unmarried** woman arriving
> **alone** at **midnight** with a **suitcase** would hardly have been
> considered **respectable**—what a wonderful difference one
> finds today! I am **grateful** to have lived to see such changes,
> because whatever old-fashioned people may say about the
> greater **decorum** and **modesty** of women in Queen Victoria's
> time, those who can remember the old conditions know how
> **difficult** and **humiliating** they were![1]

We are all grateful to have lived to see such changes, to be able to move about in the world with the same freedom as a man, both literally and metaphorically.

Those of us who have attained such freedoms, of course.

The difficulties with gender continue to arise as we are confronted with relapses like the trite and essentialist, Men are from Mars-Women are from Venus.[2] Or when the media gushes endlessly about what the First Lady of the United States, Michelle Obama, was wearing and how much it cost, or more unfortunately about the size of her bare arms.

Much more serious are the official statements that not only refuse equality between the sexes but continue relentlessly to construct the sexes in opposition to each other. It becomes doubly difficult for women when they are misunderstood in this way by their religious leaders. It is still humiliating for Catholic women to be told by Pope John Paul II, Pope Benedict XVI and Pope Francis I, that they alone have a 'special' and caring nature, one that best fits them for work in the home and the raising of children.[3] Once again, we are confronted

---

1. *Strong Poison*, 190
2. John Gray, *Men are from Mars-Women are from Venus* (New York: Harper Collins, 1994).
3. Pope Benedict XVI 'Letter to the Bishops of the Catholic Church on the Collaboration of Men and Women in the Church and in the World', Rome, 31 May 2004.

with the danger of collapsing the terms 'sex' and 'gender': only the female (the word that denotes our sex) is naturally predisposed (meaning born that way) to be nurturing (a socially constructed feminine practice and virtue). Men should also find it insulting to learn that they were not born with this innate ability to care for their children. At best, it seems, they can only mimic the care that they see their wives provide.

It is still humiliating for the Muslim Shi'ite women of Afghanistan, who live in areas controlled by the Taliban, to be denied an education, or to be told in Iran, in terms of the Code of Civil Law, that their worth is only half that of a man. It is much more than humiliating to be subjected to the horrors of a clitorodectomy so that his sexual pleasure will be enhanced and she won't be tempted to wander. And, it is still humiliating for Israeli women to be pushed to the back of the bus, subjected to insults and humiliation simply for being female because the ultra-Orthodox are demanding sex based separation in public transport.[4]

Finally, gender talk can be dangerous if it dilutes the social and economic aspects of the political agenda of feminism. When we use the word gender in place of feminist, we risk selling out on the goal of equality. Gender describes the current configuration of the sexes; it tells us the way things are but not how they ought to be. Feminism is a revolution that wants to overturn the *status quo*. Too often, we find that in the European Union or the United Nations it is far more acceptable, more comfortable, to talk about gender because it is a nice, neutral, non-political, descriptive word.

I teach a course in a psychotherapy training program. The course is designated, 'Gender in Society, the Female Perspective'. The program also provides a course entitled, 'Gender in Society, the Male Perspective'. Obviously, we have an even-handed course director who is concerned to know how gender will influence the way in which clients construe their problems and how they enact solutions. I tell the students that the course should be called 'Feminist Psychotherapy' because I want more than even-handed. Even-handed is not what it purports to be. It is not neutral but instead is a positive endorsement of the *status quo*. I want equality and to get that the students need to

---

4. See, Alexander Efimov, 'Israel and Creeping Segregation', NEO (New Eastern Outlook) 4th December, 2014.

know that men and women still do not come either to marriage or the work place on equal terms. I know, equal pay for equal work will arrive at any moment and so will adequate creche facilities—that are, incidentally, still presumed to be something that only women need.

Conventional courtesies aim, all unwittingly, to undermine the revolution. These are the ways in which a gentleman treats a lady. A lady may pick up the pieces after a battle, may bind the wounds of the combatants but she won't lead the revolution. Indeed, as Wimsey reminds us while punting with Harriet in Oxford:

> *Would you now prefer to be independent and take the pole?*
> *I admit that it is better fun to punt than be punted, and a*
> *desire to have all the fun is nine-tenths of the law of chivalry.*[5]

When we are examining the relationship of Harriet Vane and Peter Wimsey we have, under the magnifying glass, a heterosexual relationship in which power counts heavily because it is mostly distributed in a way that favours the man over the woman. If Peter has more power than Harriet, was he born superior? No. Is it merely a coincidence? Definitely not. Could it be a matter of personal preference? Well, it could be for him but it certainly won't be for her. It seems certain that he prefers the status quo because it is only women who have been pressing for a change in gender-stereotypical relations at least since Sayers began writing her novels eighty years ago.

---

5. *Gaudy Night*, 345

'Do you know any man who sincerely admires a woman for her brains?'

'Well', said Harriet, 'certainly not many.'

'You may think you know **one**,' said Miss Hillyard with a bitter emphasis. 'Most of us think at some time or other that we know **one**. But the man usually has some other little axe to grind.'

'Very likely,' said Harriet. 'You don't seem to have a very high opinion of men—of the male character, I mean, as such.'

'No,' said Miss Hillyard, 'not very high. But they have an admirable talent for imposing their point of view on society in general. All women are sensitive to male criticism. Men are not sensitive to female criticism. They despise the critics.'

Gaudy Night

Chapter 2
Reason: And Intuition

Conventional wisdom has it that women do not actually reason, they intuit. For a long time now, a millennia or two anyway, men claimed that they were the primary repository of the human ability to reason, at least of the fully formed variety. Women, they told us, do have brains but the functioning of the female brain is seriously impaired by the fact that the 'fair sex', read more beautiful but not as bright, is also a jumbled bundle of emotions and intuitions. Quite simply, emotions get in the way of clear thinking. For goodness sake, stop being so emotional. Stop crying. Can't you think straight? Therefore, when it comes to the ostensibly human ability to reason, men, who always think straight and dread emotion, and are, of course, not permitted to cry, are superior to women. Women, being associated with body, with birth, with lactating, have at least one foot in the chaotic, unpredictable, irrational world of nature.

As Miss Hillyard points out, there are not many men who admire women for their brains. She too has been taught that women are not to concern themselves with the realm of ideas. Their role is not to think, create, imagine, shape, govern, decide, invest, conquer or to point the way to God. No, women's role is better described as a function, the natural function of the reproductive body. She is immanent not transcendent. Her body is both her definition and her destiny.

But what if—and here is a wild speculation—women were as rational as men? And what if women, traditionally the sex who were to tend to the needs of others, to nurture and care, to be the minders of intimate relationships while their men were empire building, became the experts in the cultivation and expression of human emotions? What if they harnessed this experiential knowledge to the power of their brains and brought all this to bear on problem solving? If they did, then women would have the power of the mind, as well as the emotions and feminine intuition, to bring to the stage of ethical decision making.

With double the resources utilised by men, women would be much better equipped, and therefore much more likely to arrive at the right, the better, the more ethically comprehensive answer. For example, the place is Ireland, the year is 1847. At the height of the Great Hunger, Tom is angered at the sight of his landlord's fat belly and grief-stricken at the sight of his children's grass stained lips. Overcome by both emotions, he steals a turnip to feed them. When Tom is judged by the law and reason alone he is transported as thief to Australia. When he is judged with compassion, this father is given a second turnip.

Why, we might even say that until men learn to *think* with their *feelings* as women already do, until they learn to live within the equation that Reason + Emotion = Best Possible Solution, then women are more rational than men!

When a woman arrives at a solution more quickly than a man, he may at least denigrate it, if not dismiss it entirely, as being the result of mere feminine intuition. Her solution couldn't have been based on reason; if it had, he would have arrived at it just as quickly as she did. Men have tended to have a great deal of difficulty in thinking of women as rational as themselves, and they have always disparaged feminine intuition. Not enough data, they say. In *Have His Carcase*, Sayers tells us that Inspector Umpeltey laughed at one possible explanation of the case, saying:

> Miss Vane's intuition, as they call it, is against it.'

To which Harriet retorted,

> 'It's not intuition . . . There's no such thing. It's
> common sense.'

The difficulty that now confronted men like Inspector Umpeltey was that women like Harriet Vane so often arrived at the right response or the more complete solution, and so they had to find a way to account for this. They had to find a label for this feminine process;

they couldn't call it reason because that is what men do and women could not be seen to reason more effectively than men. So they called it feminine intuition, something that only women do. Not finding its basis solely in reason, it is almost as if women come up with the right answer by pure chance or good luck.

What is this thing that men name feminine intuition? To start with, I think Sayers is right, it is not intuition but common sense. Intuition has been defined as something we know immediately, without having to go through a process of conscious reasoning. But it is not luck that brings women to the correct prediction but rather the long, common sense process of spending a lot of time practicing or paying attention. We reach that point of immediacy when we do something often, gaining knowledge through repetition. Then our response looks intuitive, a practical and coherent reaction to common needs and situations. Women observe and engage, pay attention and respond within the myriad varieties of human relationships that are the fabric of our personal, emotional lives. They spend their lives gathering data, then they put together this huge mass of human responses, sort and sift them and come up with answers. These answers are not the result of pure chance or good luck. This is common sense, which finds its foundation in paying attention to the needs of others. This is the practice of attentiveness.

I don't think it matters which label you attach to this skill, intuition or common sense so long as you recognise that it is a skill and a skill that is heightened in its development in women because women practice paying attention to the needs of others. That is what they have been taught by their mothers to do. Caring for others is our cultural hallmark of the good woman. It was not chance that accounted for women developing this talent; it arose out of being excluded from the academy and government. All the time that men had been governing states, leading armies, learning to build bridges and blow glass, women were confined to the home and the task of child raising. A woman's world and a woman's work were tied to the web of intimate relationships and intimate relationships only work when you pay attention to the needs of others.

Second, and note carefully, this talent can be developed and perfected with practice, which leads us to another wild speculation— intuition or common sense is equally available to men. As William

Ickes, Professor of Psychology at the University of Texas tells us, women are not born better able than men to read people, 'studies have shown that the difference isn't in ability but in motivation'.[1]

But then things changed. Women began to be fed-up, angry and impatient at their confinement. It is more an accurate description than misplaced irony to remember that a woman's pregnancy would be called her confinement. So women began to march. They started to point out the injustices in this bifurcated system, where he was mind and she was body; he was cooly rational and clear headed and she was that jumbled bundle of emotional responses. They argued, cajoled, reasoned, pleaded, petitioned, reasoned some more, agitated again and then, finally, they got the vote and jury duty. It was a beginning.

Then a funny thing happened. A great deal had changed and very little had changed. Try this example from Sayers in Strong Poison where a male law clerk opines in a conversation with Wimsey:

> 'But juries are very unreliable, especially nowadays, with
> women on them. We see a good deal of the fair sex in this
> profession,' said the clerk, with a sly smile 'and very few
> of them are remarkable for possessing the legal mind' . . .
> 'I'm an old fashioned man—the ladies were most adorable
> when they adorned and inspired and did not take any active
> part in affairs'.[2]

Women get put on juries then juries become especially unreliable? This is not a fact, it is a perception and this is where the trouble really starts. Take, for example, a fascinating study conducted in the United States in 2009. It was conducted by David R Hekman and his colleagues at the University of Wisconsin, Milwaukee, and what they discovered helps to explain why white men still earn twenty-five percent more than equally well-performing women and minorities. The team studied an employee/customer encounter in a bookstore. It was found that people will give higher customer satisfaction ratings to white men than to women and members of racial minorities even when their performance is the same. Although there were substantial numbers of women (forty-five percent) and non-whites (forty-one

---

1. Kylstra, Carolyn, 'Yes, You Can Read a Woman's Mind', in *Men's Health* http://www.menshealth.com/men/sex-relationships.
2. *Strong Poison*, 82.

percent) in each of the study groups, the interviewees were nineteen percent more satisfied with the white man's performance. They were even more satisfied with the stores cleanliness and appearance when the employee was a white man.[3] In a second test, some 12,000 patients in a health maintenance plan rated white male doctors as more approachable and competent than equally well-performing women or minority doctors. Still, today, we might expand Miss Hillyard's question and ask, do we know any man or woman who sincerely admires a woman for her brains?

What these studies tells us is that sexism and racism are alive and well. Someone is still defining what is best and brightest and it looks like that might be white men. Sexual and racial prejudice run deep. Very deep. You can ensure equality of educational opportunity, pass employment equality legislation, even (in fairy land) enforce equal rates of pay but sex and racial bias persist. These biases were deep-rooted when Sayers was writing in the 1930s and still we cannot dig them out.

How do you change customer biases? Apparently the answer is, very slowly. Across all twenty-seven nation states of the European Union one more attempt has just begun. This is a program designed to educate all citizens on the equal value of women. The perceived need for such a program is in itself staggering in the light of the anti-feminist backlash that claims that feminism as both a philosophy and a political program is *passé*. Despite this claim, The European Institute for Gender Equality was established in 2006 at the *request* of both the European Council and the European Parliament; it was to become operational by 2008; its first Director, Virginija Langbakk was appointed in 2009.[4] The mission statement of this Institute is 'to fight discrimination based on sex', a clear recognition of the unequal treatment of half the European population.

The Roadmap for Equality between Men and Women, 2006–2010 is designed to drive forward the same equality agenda for which feminism has been agitating for over half a century. As a collective movement, second wave feminism was building upon the foundations

---

3. David R Hekman and colleagues (2009) 'An Examination of Whether and How Racial and Gender Biases Influence Customer Satisfaction', in *Academy of Management Journal*, 53/2, April 2010.
4. For full details of the Institute see http://europa.eu/legislation.

laid by the individual efforts of women like Dorothy Sayers who began her personal campaign thirty years before even though, like many women today, she did not want to call herself a feminist.

This Roadmap identifies six priority areas:

First, economic independence for women and men when women still suffer the effects of a fifteen percent pay gap.

Second, the reconciliation of private and professional life, where women are still doing most of the child care and where few men take parental leave or work part-time.

Third, equal representation in decision-making, the initial aim being to reach a target of twenty-five percent of women in leading public-sector positions.

Fourth, the eradication of all forms of gender based violence, such as female genital mutilation, early or forced marriages and the trafficking of women.

Fifth, the elimination of gender stereotypes in the areas of education and culture, in the labour market and in the media.

And finally, sixth, the promotion of gender equality in external and development policies in an effort to reaffirm the statement of the 'European Consensus on Development' that gender equality is one of the five key principles of development policy.

The very need for this document, and the laying out of each of the six elements contained therein, attests to the fact that in the allegedly culturally civilised and politically liberal first world, women's minds and bodies are still less valued than those of men.

Paying attention to women's morality, one which draws upon the emotions to pay careful attention to the needs of others, and insists upon intuitive or common sense solutions, can go a long way towards the implementation of this Agenda.

If you hear anyone suggest to you that we live in a post-feminist world, one in which men and women, reason and the emotions, are equally valued, then I can only suggest that you refer them to the governors of Europe and the heads of its twenty-seven member states.

'I only wish I could help you.'

'You can. If only you would. I'm sure you're clever. You look clever. I'm not clever. I do wish I was. I think I should have been happier if I was clever. It must be nice to **do** things. I've often thought that if I could have painted pictures or ridden a motor-cycle or something, I should have got more out of life'.

Harriet agreed, gravely, that it was perhaps a good thing to have an occupation of some sort.

'But of course,' said Mrs. Weldon, 'I was never brought up to that. I have lived for my emotions. I can't help it. I suppose I am made that Way . . . If only he had been kinder to me, I could have lived **in** and **for** him.'

Have His Carcase

Chapter 3
Emotions: This Woman's Work

In my work as a psychotherapist, the story is so common that it is frightening. Are we all so alike? More or less, with hardly any variation, I hear:

> 'We got on so well in the beginning. He used to call me all the time, every night or at least a text. Most days he would phone me at work. He always wanted to know what I was doing, he was interested. He was so loving and he listened to me, really listened. We would sit and talk for hours and hours at a time. He was really thoughtful, you know, going out of his way to do things for me. We were so happy.'

Every good story has a beginning, a middle and an end. The middle of this one is a slide. He calls less frequently, gets a glazed look in his eye when she talks about her day with the kids or the girlfriends or the latest problem in the school. They now talk less and he forgets anniversaries. They argue a lot about housework and child care. She is not happy and he doesn't seem to notice.

The story ends in my office. We have reached the point where she states, like most people who come for marital therapy, that they have 'communication problems', the most commonly stated complaint of couples whose marriages end in divorce. She is feeling utterly frustrated by the fact that she 'can't get through to him'. Listening, as every psychotherapist will tell you, is the major component of good communication. How did we get to the point when he stops listening? Well, maybe because what he is hearing most of the time now is criticism. He is sitting in my office saying to her, 'I love you. What's the problem?' She is saying, 'You say you love me, but it doesn't feel like it over here. The problem is that if you listened to me, you would know. The real problem is that you don't show it.' Or, as Mark Twain put it, actions speak louder than words but not nearly as often.

What has happened of course, and here I will give you my own shorthand version of events, is that he has wooed and won his fair lady, installed her in the house, secured his progeny, and gone back to the market place. She may well have gone back to work too, but for what follows this does not make any difference. When he comes in at night, to his 'haven in a heartless world' as Christopher Lasch described it, he is 'too tired' to talk. He listens, but without asking for the details, which is a sure sign of lack of interest. Yet, she remembers very clearly just how it was with them in the beginning—all the emotional engagement and attentive caring. Not too surprisingly, she still hankers after this loving partner and so she has been figuratively beating on his chest for years, saying 'come out, come out, wherever you are. I know you are in there!'

What I am particularly interested to explore here is the notion that these two people are really not so different from any of us. Certainly, they have decided to talk over their differences with someone like me but there are lots of other couples out there, going around in ever decreasing circles, who would benefit from an open and honest conversation together. It might be painful, but it is better than the accretion of one unhappy incident piled on top of another until the pair run out of hope completely and think that divorce is, if not a desirable outcome, at least a necessary relief. Perhaps a better way to view their situation is to see it as a variation on the theme of conflict experienced by so many couples.

Let us rewind the tape. How did young love unravel until she found herself at the point of being unhappily married and letting him know it? One possible answer has been provided by Mrs Weldon: '*I have lived for my emotions. I can't help it. I suppose I am made that way.*' A lot of people are quite sure that women are more emotional than men (just as they are sure men are more interested in sex than women). But they never stop to ask, are they born that way or have they been given permission by the culture to act that way?

Answers to this question have been provided by two very different sources, Nancy Chodorow[1] and Pope John Paul II[2]. Even as they come at the problem from different angles and with a different purpose, they both maintain that women have a 'special nature', one that is gentle and nurturing. However, the fundamental difference between them is that while the Pope says women are born with a special nature, Chodorow's psychological theory says that women have learned to behave differently. This theoretical divergence has huge ramifications because while the former is unchangeable, the latter contains within it the promise of new life for both sexes.

Chodorow argues that boys raised by women—which is nearly all of them—must eventually, if they are ever to acquire their masculine gender identity, reject mother and all that she stands for: love, tenderness, sensitivity and vulnerability. He loves her but he has to leave her, and all that she represents, in the quest to differentiate himself and become a man. For the little girl the situation is just the reverse. Her identification with her mother as her gender role model provides the very basis for her feminine identity. Where he is confronted with a developmental hurdle on the road to manhood she is off to a flying start in the formation of her identity.

In the act of rejecting mother and all things feminine, boys are forever wary about expressing their emotions or being the ones to do the daily care-giving. They fight to free themselves from the feminine so their friends won't call them sissy and in that very act of denial they lose half their human potential. They don't engage in emotional friendships with other men and they find it equally hard to trust themselves to another woman or to be dependent on her because too often it was their mother, their first love, who threw them out of the nest for fear of doing harm to their young masculinity. Naturally, because their father was brought up the same way, they also lack a masculine role model who does the love work in the home. As a result, Chodorow argues, gender stereotypes are born and reproduced again and again in family after family. As we know, men feel just as entitled to receive care from their wives as they did from their mothers. Their problem is giving it, reciprocating it, because if they do they are in

---

1. Nancy Chodorow, *The Reproduction of Mothering: Psychoanalysis and the Sociology of Gender* (University of California Press, 1978).
2. Pope John Paul II, Apostolic Letter *Mulieris Dignitatem*. Rome, 15 August 1988.

danger of looking like mother, a woman, a sissy and, worst of all, they risk becoming dependent on their wives. It is worth noting that just as our denial of our dependency on the natural world has become the source of our environmental problems, so men's denial of dependence upon women is the source of the problems in relationships.

For Chodorow, the only way to break this cycle, which is damaging to both sexes, is for men to assume equal responsibility for the daily, hands on, tasks of house work and parenting, what we can call love labour. This does not mean that they have to actually do it, any more than she does, but they have to be equally responsible to see that it is done. Parenting has got to start meaning half mum and half dad, a role and a job that is equally shared.

There is another way to break this cycle, which we will talk more about later, and that is for women to change. Where men have to start doing what they are not doing (paying more attention to her needs), women have to stop doing what they are doing (paying too little attention to their own needs). By this I mean, women have to start thinking about what it is they want out of life and how they are going to make it happen. What has been called the burned chop syndrome, where she takes the smallest and least attractive portion of the evening meal, has to stop.

A few qualifications are necessary here. This psychological theory has a very practical drawback. It does not explain how difficult it will be to get men to take on the emotional tasks in the family if they have learned to be, as the psychotherapeutic jargon puts it, physically and emotionally peripheral. It will be doubly difficult in traditional families where he goes out to work and she stays in to work. And, it is not helped where she works outside the home but does the double shift, or works part-time and still does the double shift. These are situations in which gender roles are entrenched. Nonetheless, some fathers are doing more parenting, although they still do much less housework, and this presence must surely add up over time to a positive role model for little boys. In the same way, there are many households now headed by women only and single women tend to treat their children equally.

Our hope lies in the feminist movement which is still, as it always has been, advocating equality in thought and action. What we are aiming towards is a '**Mr** Weldon' who can say, quite happily, with no sense of being emasculated, with no trace of an identity crisis, with no hint of being out of step with the rest of his sex, and most definitely without his tongue in his cheek, that 'I have lived for my emotions . . . *I could have lived in and for her*', but this time with mutual reciprocity. This should not represent the sum total of his activities any more than it should represent the sum total of hers. Recall the burnt chop. Living for someone is only one of the things we do—we also paint pictures and ride motor cycles. Harriet agrees that we all need *'an occupation of some sort'*.

As I suggested above, it will not be easy for men to learn to express their emotions because both sexes were brought up to be aware that our feelings might 'run away with us', or 'get in the way of clear thinking'. Emotions, we were all taught, were just plain dangerous because they spelt the death or destruction of rational thought. To have an illuminating thought is wondrous; to experience an outburst of emotion is a handicap.

What we desire is a marriage in which he reverts to what we know he knows, those behaviours she experienced when they first met. What is required is continuity, so that when courtship turns to marriage he still responds with emotional labour for his wife, one where he listens, tells her she's wonderful, bolsters her self-confidence, cheers her successes and soothes her disappointments: the kinds of things that women do for their husbands all their married lives. One in which he says, 'I know you've had a hard day, sit there and I'll get the dinner'. Or, 'No, I'll stay with the children, you go and have a game of golf'. And, 'Don't forget its your mother's birthday next week'. Why is that so amazing?

Hard as it will be for men to unlearn the inadequate behaviours they were taught there is no earthly reason why this cannot happen: if they can get to the moon they can surely make it as far as the kitchen, the laundry and the nursery. It is both untrue and insulting to say that men are born incapable of caring to the same degree as women. Care is a human virtue not a female one. Men have been gendered to deny or suppress their emotions. Women have been gendered to express their emotions in all their variety. But men weren't born without hearts any more than women were born without brains.

Men may have to learn from women for a period, learn all that she has learned over centuries of being the one in charge of relationships, learn to express their emotions and learn to enjoy the intimacies of friendship that stretch them beyond discussing football or politics over a beer. As the Director of the Australian Shedding Movement put it: 'Men don't talk face to face; they talk shoulder to shoulder when they are working on a job together.' Well, men need to learn to talk face to face. Then they would no longer be reduced to one intimate companion and would not be so desperately lonely on retirement or if widowed; he too would have a circle of knowing friends to turn to.

For men to willingly give up their currently entrenched male privilege of the one being ministered to would expand their humanity and happiness exponentially.

We now know that child care and housework are things that women do but it is not who women *are* of their very natures. We can no longer tolerate the 'Mr Weldons' who claim, 'I can't help it. I suppose I am made that way' any more than we can tolerate that definition of a woman. Being an emotional, as well as a rational, human being is of the essence of both men and women. It seems only fair, just, intelligent and in accordance with all observable reality to claim that neither sex has been born an emotional or a rational cripple. Both sexes, as Sayers tells us over and over again, are equally capable of being fully human.

'Are you fond of children, madam?'

'Oh, yes', said Harriet. Actually, she did not care much about children; but one can hardly say so, bluntly, to those possessed of these blessings.

'You ought to be married and have some of your own, madam. There! I oughtn't to have said that—it's not my place. But it seems to me a dreadful thing to see all these unmarried ladies living together. It isn't natural, is it?'

'Well, Annie, it's all according to taste. And one has to wait for the right person to come along.'

'That's very true, madam . . . But it seems a great shame to keep up this big place just for women to study books in. I can't see what girls want with books. Books won't teach them to be good wives.'

'What dreadful opinions!' said Harriet.

Gaudy Night

Chapter 4
A Woman's Place is in the Home

Alice Landry was born in England in 1950. She married Louis Carroll in 1970 and he installed her in the home which he had bought on a loan that only he was entitled to apply for. She took his name and became Mrs. Louis Carroll and had his children. She is now subsumed by the roles of wife and mother. As Mrs Louis Carroll, and John and Mary's mum, Alice has disappeared. He is the head of the household and because she was married before 1 January 1974, the effective date of the Domicile and Matrimonial Proceedings Act, 1973, she was his legal dependent and unable to acquire a domicile of her own choice. That famous English jurist, Lord Denning, MR, described the married woman's domicile of dependency as 'the last barbarous relic of a wife's servitude' (*Gray v Formosa [1963] p.259,267*). Even so, while a wife was finally able to choose her own legal domicile after 1974 that other barbarous relic of a wife's servitude, spousal rape, was not recognised by the English courts until the 1991 decision of the House of Lords in *R v R (All ER 481)*.

Moving westward, across the Irish Sea we find the situation no different. Article 41.2 of the Irish Constitution makes it clear that a woman's proper place is the home:

> In particular, the State recognises that by her life within the home, woman gives to the State a support without which the common good cannot be achieved. The State shall, therefore, endeavour to ensure that mothers shall not be obliged by economic necessity to engage in labour to the neglect of their duties in the home.

You might object that, being written in 1937, this Article simply reflected the mores of the times in which Sayers lived. But it is still the law of the land and it is still impacting the lives of Irish women, especially psychologically. By implying that the natural place of women is in the home, it is propounding the grossest form of sexual stereotyping. As we have now discovered in respect to amendments to the law of domicile, a woman's place is a woman's choice.

Conventional wisdom, which both generates and justifies constitutional clauses like Article 41.2, holds that if you, a mother, do not stay home with the children then the welfare of everyone in the country, the common good, will somehow suffer. That is a heavy ideological burden to bear and it is one that is laid upon women only and it is laid upon them continuously. If teenagers are delinquent it is because their mothers did not stay home with them. If marriages break down it is because women went out to work and became financially independent. If old people are not taken back home but left in hospitals it is because the mother is not available in the home to provide daily care for them. If young men commit suicide it is because young women are showing them up at school or in the business world. Yet surely the common good unravels if fathers are so consumed at work that they do not notice that their child is staying out too late and drinking too much. It cannot be good for marriages if a husband is having an affair with a work colleague. What happens to common decency, what message is conveyed to the next generation, if men fail to bring their aging parents home from hospital to care for them?

The phrase Common Good, like the word Commonwealth, is the product of religious institutions. It has been defined as 'the sum total of social conditions which allow *people*, either as groups or as individuals, to reach their fulfilment more freely and more easily'.[1] But in this context, as in so many others, it tends to be the interests of men, not 'people', that are fostered and protected so that they may flourish.

Why has Ireland not amended the Constitution to read: 'The state shall, therefore, endeavour to ensure that *parents* shall not be obliged by economic necessity to engage in labour to the neglect of their duties at home'. That would remove entirely any psychological burden while at the same time making it possible for all citizens,

---

1. *Gaudium et Spes (The Joy and the Hope)* n 26. See Abbott, *The Documents of the Second Vatican Council.*

both male and female, to understand that their home duties are their shared responsibility. It would certainly reflect the mores of these times, where two thirds of Irish women are already in the workforce. Furthermore, it seems reasonable to assume that many more women would be working outside the home if the husbands and fathers were doing their half share within it. And the pressure is building. Irish research predicts that: 'By 2012, women are forecast to form the majority of business, financial and legal professionals, and the proportion of managers who are women will almost reach the proportion of women in the workforce as a whole.'[2]

Moving further west again, across 'the pond' of the Atlantic Ocean, the Constitution of the United States proclaims that 'all men are created equal', a statement that did not include a black man or indeed a woman of any colour. Even here, even today, in liberal, democratic, wealthy America, women, as a class, are still not treated equally. Furthermore, a simple but comprehensive example will suffice to point out the problem of inequality between the sexes in all three countries that we have highlighted here: England, Ireland and the United States. This example is the Global Gender Gap Report, 2009, produced by the World Economic Forum, studying 134 countries and representing ninety percent of the world's population. This report rests on four pillars, examining the gap between men and women in the fundamental categories of economic participation and opportunity, educational attainment, political empowerment and health and survival. On these measures Ireland ranks eighth, the United Kingdom fifteenth and the United States of America thirty-first. In the United States, the overall labour force participation of women is sixty-nine percent but only fifty-six percent of women are represented among professional and technical workers. The report states:

> Over the past few decades, both developed and developing countries have made substantial progress in educating women and improving their health outcomes. In many developed countries, women now account for more than half of the college and university graduates, and many developing

---

2. Dr Pete Lunn, 'How the Irish Workforce Will Look in 2012', in The Economic and Social Research Institute, Ireland, 2 August, 2007.

countries have dramatically reduced gender gaps in literacy and primary/secondary education.

Yet even in developed countries whose dependence on knowledge industries and knowledge workers is large and growing, *there are still **significant gaps** in the job opportunities for women and in the wages paid to women compared with their male counterparts,* and these gaps are even larger in most developing countries. (Italics and emphasis added).

The stark conclusion of this almost universal research project is that, 'No country in the world has achieved gender equality'.

The world, it seems, still agrees with Annie that real love means 'sticking to your man through thick and thin and putting up with everything'. Only the good woman realises that 'books won't teach them to be good wives' but that she must do what comes naturally: 'to cook his meals and mend his clothes and bear his children . . .'

If there is universal discrimination against women in the public world of paid work, it is not difficult to conclude that this injustice emanates from the deeply held belief that a woman's proper place is within the home. This ideological stance directly results in its pragmatic counterpart: earning less than her male partner, it is obvious that she is the one who should put in the hours at home and take primary responsibility for its smooth functioning.

When they both say, 'But, I have a meeting scheduled . . .', it is mostly the mother who will have to back down and attend the parent and teacher meeting, or collect the sick child early from school. If members of the immediate or extended family, young or old, become ill then she is most frequently the one who will have to give up her paid employment to become the primary carer. In the United Kingdom, The Work and Families Act of 2006, provided workers with the right to *request* flexible working hours to care for aged or infirm members of their immediate or extended family. It can come as no real surprise to learn that ninety percent of those who opted to apply for such leave were women.

The fact that women are paid less for the same work is a glaring injustice and we will tackle that again in a later chapter. But there are several attendant ideas that float around in a subterranean kind of way because it is politically incorrect to say them out loud. Is she paid less because she is less rational and therefore less able? Does a male colleague sexually harass her because he resents her presence, or in the hope that he will drive her out of the office or at least intimidate her? Or, is she a threat because she might take a job that a man could otherwise profit from? Annie is certainly angry about that idea. She would like to burn down Harriet's university college 'and all places like it, where you teach women to take men's jobs'.

Today, we still get a very clear signal that a woman's place is in the home when we turn the spotlight on the confusing area of maternity, paternity and parental leave. In broad outline, the UK provides for one year of paid maternity leave, Ireland for eighteen weeks while in the USA there is no national program at all although cash benefits might be provided at the state level.

For the fathers of these babies, the UK provides for two weeks paid leave, whereas in Ireland there is still no legislative or statutory entitlements for fathers to paid paternity leave although both parents are legally entitled to unpaid parental leave. In the USA, it is a case of every man for himself if he wants to seek time with his newborn.

The fact is that the majority of men are themselves anxious about paternity leave—but perhaps for the wrong reasons. They worry that even a request to the boss will look like lack of commitment. They know the stories about who is last in the office at night, whose is the last car in the car park. They fear loss of income, advancement, benefits and bonuses and not least the scorn of their fellow male workers. Caring for infants is 'woman's work'. Which is not entirely their fault as nobody has ever taught them anything different. I can remember when my first child was born and all the women friends came to visit and help; they were all at ease, comfortable and confident around babies. My husband said he 'felt like a red Indian circling the wagons; he couldn't find a way in'. However, he was looking, and although it was a time of dis-ease and discomfort for him, over time, he learned how to do it all.

The notion that because women produce the children then they are the ones to care for them is pervasive. That's natural, we hear over and over. Womenandchildren is one word. Which is why we have maternity leave. It is never long enough, nor is the remuneration adequate. While we blithely repeat that 'the family is the basic unit of society', politicians and trade union officials will tell you that business groups always oppose any extension of maternity benefits as well as the introduction of paternity leave. They will tell you that it is too expensive, too hard to arrange and that the economy cannot cope with it, especially in times of recession. They overlook the fact that mothers have to keep coping when apparently the economy cannot.

What is so unnatural about fatherhood? And how is it, that in this area, men seem to have overlooked the need to legislate to provide this right for themselves? Could it possibly be that they don't want it?

If we are ever going to achieve equality between the sexes two things need to happen and they must both be the subject of enforceable legislation: Women must receive equal pay and men must be obliged to take paternity leave. If women are doing their share in the market place then men must do their share at home. 'What dreadful opinions!' said Harriet.

'Though I am afraid,' added Miss Lydgate, 'We may have to lose Annie from this staircase . . . But then, poor thing, she is a widow with two small children , and really ought not to have to be in service at all. Her husband . . . went out of his mind . . . and died or shot himself . . . leaving her very badly off so she was glad to take what she could. The little girls are boarded out with Mrs Jukes . . . so Annie is able to go and see them at the week-ends. It is nice for her and brings in a little extra for Mrs Jukes.'

'Poor Jukes,' said Miss Lydgate . . . 'He got into sad trouble and we were obliged to dismiss him. He turned out to be not quite honest, I am sorry to say. But we found him work as a jobbing gardener . . . However, we made a small loan to his wife, to pay off his debts, and they certainly repaid it most honestly . . . '

'You've lost Agnes, too, I see.'

'Yes . . . She began to find work too much for her and had to retire. I'm glad to say we were able to squeeze out a tiny pension for her—only a trifle, but as you know, our income has to be stretched very carefully to cover everything. And we arranged a little scheme by which she takes in odd jobs of mending and so on for the students and attends to the College linen. It all helps; and she's especially glad because that crippled sister of hers can do part of the work and contribute something to their small income. Agnes says the poor soul is so much happier now that she need not feel herself a burden.'

Harriet marvelled, not for the first time, at the untiring conscientiousness of administrative women. Nobody's interests ever seemed to be overlooked or forgotten, and an endless goodwill made up for a perennial shortage of funds.

Gaudy Night

Chapter 5
Care: Love's Labour Lost

Who cares? Or is it, who cares, who cares? The answer to the first question is women. The answer to the second is men. She takes care of him and he really cares that she will keep doing it. She knows that this is her job, to be in charge of the emotional component of the relationship, to nurture it, to fuel it and, if it goes wrong, to take responsibility for repairing it. That is why it is almost always women who initiate therapy. He always wants to try and sort it out at home, on their own, because he is not as comfortable with the language of the personal, the emotional, the intimate. He too knows that it is her job to nourish the relationship. What takes place in private, what is part of their in-house life together, is, by definition, women's work. In fact, we have arrived at the point where both sexes tacitly agree that this is just the way things are.

Why is it that so many of us think that this is just the way things are? Probably because it is an observable reality. But where did this 'reality' come from? We know that this trait is not innate, that women were not born more caring than men, just as men were not born more rational than women. Caring is learned behaviour.

In this chapter, I am talking about emotional caregiving. The kind of caring that is not paid for as a commodity. The kind of caring that cannot be financially quantified, or transferable, like housework. The kind of caring that Harriet describes as being done by women, with 'untiring conscientiousness' and 'endless goodwill' that goes into making sure that the 'interests' or needs of others are met. The kind of caring that is also described as being empathic, understanding, loving, listening, soothing, available, selfless, tolerant, committed, responsible, you get the idea. Yes, that sounds like 'women's work'.

Even if there was not 'a perennial shortage of funds', this kind of caring cannot be bought but the time is always made to provide it.

And, she had better find the time, too. Adult children in therapy engage in a lot of mother blaming. They are very angry with mothers who do not pay them enough attention, give them enough loving. They are never as angry with fathers. When he comes up short on the time and attention scale it is dismissed as just the way men are. It looks as if everyone concerned, husband/father, mother/wife, children, all agree—this is just the way things are. They all hold the erroneous belief that this is a state of nature.

But it is not a state of nature, at least not for one sex only. Care is a human virtue and capability, not only a female one. It is certainly true that the work of emotional care-giving is one of the things that women *do* but it is not who they *are*. It is a clever manoeuver for men to say, 'you do it, dear; you are so much better at it than I am'. Men are just as capable as women of emotional care-giving; all they need is permission from other men to do it and then they need to put in the hours to perfect the skill.

As relational beings, every man knows that it is friends and loved ones who bring happiness, warmth and joy into our lives. Every time a friend seeks us out we know that they value our company. When they don't call, we hurt. When an adult child wants to spend time with her parents, the parents feel appreciated and still wanted. When an adult child never calls or writes the sense of loss is savage. When a husband calls his wife at lunch time to say, 'just thinking of you', she obviously feels cared for. Being cared for is not only essential to our survival, it is also an essential ingredient of our development and of our well-being.

The corollary, of course, is that we do not function well, in fact, we function very poorly, when we are deprived of human contact and emotional support. That is why prisons really are punishment blocks and solitary confinement is intolerable. When we are denied love and care in our personal relationships we wither. We can say that when we are deprived of emotional care we suffer injustice because we are all entitled to the necessary conditions for our flourishing. In fact, we can go further and say that to care and be cared for are the axes of rotation around which every healthy relationship turns.

The importance of emotional care-giving becomes most obvious when it is absent. This fact is the basis for nearly all the referrals to psychotherapy practices around the world. Yes, men with jobs are under pressure to work hard to keep them. Men without jobs are under pressure to secure one. Women, with or without jobs, or working part-time for money are under the most pressure as 'a woman's work is never done'. There is no factory horn to sound the end of her working day. And, yet, whatever the employment situation of both of them, it is still the women who are doing nearly all the emotional caring. For men it is difficult to achieve a decent work/life balance; for women it is practically impossible.

It is the reciprocity of caring behaviour that is so important. We know the age old cry of children, "it's not fair!". And we are forever telling our children that they must learn to share. The importance of both fairness and sharing means that not only is it not healthy for her to be left with all the love labour in the house, it is not just. To be not merely the recipient of care but to form part of a relationship that is marked by mutual reciprocity, each one must share to a degree that is fair in the task of emotional caregiving. Within both personal and public relationships, care and justice are intertwined, one might even say, interdependent.

In modern Western democracies substantial inequalities still exist between the sexes. Fact: women are not equally represented at the highest levels of our political, financial, educational and religious institutions and there is still a higher degree of poverty for single mothers or female headed households than for single fathers. We have turned to the law and the idea of distributive justice in our attempts to remedy these situations. Even though we have had limited success we persist in our belief that a search for justice can only benefit every citizen. What we have not yet understood is that justice is a minimalist ethic. When we have given somebody their rights we have discharged our obligation to them. Where care is concerned there is almost no limit to what we can do for our neighbour; we can give to them way beyond what they might be strictly entitled to. We have been used to thinking that justice and rights are the most important aspect of our society. While they are very important, especially to those groups who are discriminated against, and those who suffer the disenfranchisement of poverty, there is a good case for saying that justice only becomes necessary to set things to rights when we have failed to care.

But justice is not only a civic or public virtue. We have to see that justice begins to operate within the privacy of the home and becomes an integral part of family life. Obviously there should be an equal distribution of labour within the home but this is also the place where children will learn about justice. Does the daughter have to do more housework and child-minding than her brother?

Political philosopher, Susan Moller Okin, puts the need for private justice with painful clarity as she outlines the stages of women's gendered reality:

> They are first set up for vulnerability during their developing years by their personal (and socially reinforced) expectations that they will be the primary caretakers of children, and that in fulfilling this role they will need to try to attract and to keep the economic support of a man, to whose work life they will be expected to give priority. They are rendered vulnerable by the actual division of labour within almost all current marriages. They are disadvantaged at work by the fact that the world of wage work, including the professions, is still largely structured around the assumption that 'workers' have wives at home. They are rendered far more vulnerable if they become the primary caretakers of children, and their vulnerability peaks if their marriages dissolve and they become single parents.[1]

Vulnerability, selflessness, generosity, trust and dependence are not out of place within marriage, because, as we have seen, they are the building blocks of emotional care-giving. However, to implement care and to avoid injustice they must be mutual; one person should not be left to be the facilitating environment for everyone. Certainly not if this means that the other person has the time to develop their capacities, to become economically and physically secure, and, finally, to become powerful enough to influence the social choices of the rest of the family.

When men fail to check in with their partners on a daily basis, when they fail to put her good, her well-being, her needs ahead of their own, when they spend no time or effort to anticipate what might give her pleasure, they are in grave danger of losing this relationship. It might not be betrayal on a grand scale, it might just trickle away over years because of a failure to make phone calls to say you will be late, or to feel free to make a unilateral decision about how you will

---

1. Susan Moller Okin, *Gender, Justice and the Family* (United States of America: Basic Books, 1989) p 139.

spend Saturday. If she has a job of any kind outside the home she may well file for divorce but even if she stays within the legal confines of the marriage, she has packed up her heart and her soul and left him. Left him to his job, to his golf, to his computer or his stamp collection—to whatever it is that she perceives is more important to him than her continual requests to help with the housework and the childcare. If your partner feels exploited or taken for granted the relationship will unravel.

The kind of caring relationships that Sayers illustrates for us through the eyes of Harriet when she returns to her Oxford College are what we might call relationships that are secondary, or once removed. College Deans are not responsible for the happiness and well-being of their staff to the same degree as are husbands, wives or partners to each other. But the identifying characteristics of emotional caring relationships are all there: Miss Lydgate is paying careful attention to the contours of the lives of the people she employs. She takes her responsibility to them seriously. She knows who is in financial trouble due to the death of one husband or the criminal behaviour of another. There is a community here, marked by over-lapping needs and interests, and she is aware of all of them. While one woman works to support her children, another minds them and benefits from the income now that her husband is earning less. While dismissing a porter for theft, she finds him another job and makes him a small loan to repay his debt. An older women is allowed to retire thanks to the provision of a small pension and a contract for the College laundry, both of which keep her and her crippled sister in money and in dignity.

Harriet marveled at Miss Lydgate and well she might. It was not simply that these staff members were provided with money, it was that the money was provided in the knowledge of what it would ease: the pain of loss, or embarrassment, or the burden of being crippled. She held gently the details of each life that had been entrusted to her. Although these were not intimate relationships, the care that Miss Lydgate administered was not a commodity; she was not paid for her attentiveness, time and sense of responsibility. She did what she did out of the goodness of her heart. She exercised a standard of care to which everyone, both male and female, can aspire. She exercised a standard of care which everyone, both male and female, can achieve by the simple expedient of being attentive to the needs of those around you.

'Well, my lord, before I was married I was barmaid at the Nine Rings, as the Chief Inspector says. Miss Montague I was then—it's a better name than Bulfinch, and I was almost sorry to say goodbye to it, but there! a girl has to make a lot of sacrifices when she marries and one more or less is nothing to signify . . . '

Strong Poison

'Excuse me, mum, wot might your married name be?'
'Lady Peter Wimsey,' said Harriet, feeling not at all sure that it was her name.

Busman's Honeymoon

Chapter 6
Identity

I had a school friend whose widowed mother remarried. On her honeymoon she made an appointment to have her hair done. Arriving early, she sat, quietly waiting. 'Mrs O'Brien', the assistant called. My friend's mother sat on. A tap on the shoulder from the assistant, 'Mrs O'Brien?'. Blushing, 'Oh, yes, dear. Of course, that's me.'

Three days ago she had been Mrs O'Kane. I do not know what her name was before she was first married but it was certainly her father's name. But whatever her name was, whatever she was called, or renamed, through each of the transitions, I have no doubt she was the same person. She was always Sheila, no matter what surname or family name she was given.

The trick is that while each of us is Sheila, we have to become Sheila, not to settle for being someone's wife and someone's mother. We are obliged to reach the fulness of our potential, to refuse to be anything other than Sheila, to be loved and respected as Sheila. And it is not always an easy trick to pull off because, as we will see, there are lots of roles out there waiting to subsume our true identity, to take us over, especially the roles of 'wife' or 'mother'.

The first, conscious hiccup in the identity story often occurs at the time of marriage. Traditionally, and still most frequently, wives take (are given?) their husband's surname. It's an interesting word, 'surname'. The Oxford dictionary says that it is a hereditary name common to all members of a family. Not a very precise definition because it is never hereditary for a wife even though it is inherited by the children of the marriage. Losing your name requires giving up much of your old identity and setting about establishing a new one. When I first heard someone say Mrs Freyne, I reacted like the new Mrs O'Brien: I looked over my shoulder for my mother in law. This new title did not belong to me. There are even people who would still address invitations to Professor and Mrs Sean Freyne. No wonder Harriet was not at all sure that 'Lady Peter Wimsey' really was her name. Lady Harriet Wimsey would have been bad enough but to lose your very own, particular name is everything from shocking to ridiculous.

Some women are delighted to take their husband's name. Most would not give it much thought at all, accepting that this was just something else that could be filed under 'It's Just the Way Things Are'. It is really a great deal more problematic than that though, isn't it? The proof lies in the fact that you cannot imagine the men taking the women's names. What if her name became the hereditary, family name and he disappeared beneath the designation Lord Harriet Vane? Lord Harriet! That sounds really ridiculous. Yet, if it is that shocking, how is it that we have become so comfortable with Lady Peter?

Could it be that while women have become resigned to being known by a man's name, a man could not tolerate being called by a woman's name? For her, it has become a custom. For him, it could never have developed into a custom because she was his property, his chattel. Which is why you are walked down the aisle by one man and handed over to another. I know, it is very romantic and these customs do not matter one bit—until you reverse them. Think about this: his mother walks him down the aisle to where another woman is waiting to receive him, to love and cherish him under the mantle of her name.

I have heard Angela Davis refer to this custom of giving up your own name as 'a little death to the self'. A point that is grimly reinforced by the powerful influence that religious men have over some religious women in the Catholic Church. As 'brides of Christ' many nuns also had their names taken from them to be replaced by a man's name. A friend of mine was known as Sister Mary Peter. If not hermaphroditic certainly a little death to the self. A death that was intended and reinforced by the heavy symbolism of lying under a funeral pall at the time of taking final vows. This was a death to the old life, the taking on of the new. With a vengeance. Men took religious names too but they were never Father Martha or Brother Cecilia.

These customs are not easy to break. Certainly, the nuns have renewed their thinking on the matter and young women too are keeping their own names, both of them, first and last names. But just as with women who marry and decide not to be known by their husband's name, they are still doing no more than keeping their father's name. There is the Sayers option: Dorothy L(eigh) Sayers was the daughter of Henry Sayers and Helen Leigh. She took these names and kept them, even after her marriage to Oswald Fleming. There remains, however, the problem of what to call your children. Even if you hyphenate your surnames that cannot last more than a generation. It is a problem with which men are going to have to engage if they want to insist that men and women are equal.

Another way in which women's identity is defined by marriage (or not) is being labelled 'Miss' or 'Mrs'. Whether he marries or not, he is always 'Mr'. If women want marital status privacy they have to opt for 'Ms'—pronounced Miz, which is a word without meaning; it is an obfuscation and it is meant to be. It becomes more clear all the time that the legalities of marriage have no impact on a man's identity. Or, as Sayers makes the point through Mrs. Bulfinch, it is the girl who 'has to make a lot of sacrifices when she marries. . .'

What are these sacrifices? And how much of the self should be sacrificed in marriage? Not too much, according to Sayers. On this she is worth quoting at length because she is vehemently egalitarian:

> 'Yes,' said Miss de Vine. 'I once got engaged to somebody. But I found I was always blundering . . . making quite elementary mistakes about him. In the end I realised that I simply wasn't taking as much trouble with him as I should have done over a disputed reading. So I decided he wasn't my job'. She smiled. 'For all that, I was fonder of him than he was of me. He married an excellent woman who is devoted to him and does make him her job . . .'
>
> 'I suppose one oughtn't to marry anybody, unless one is prepared to make him a full-time job.'
>
> 'Probably not; though there are a few rare people, I believe, who don't look on themselves as jobs but as fellow-creatures . . .'
>
> 'The worst of being a job,' said Miss de Vine, 'is the devastating effect it has on one's character. I'm very sorry for the person who is somebody else's job; he (or she, of course) ends by devouring or being devoured, either of which is bad for one . . .'
>
> 'Then you're all for the impersonal job?'
>
> 'I am', said Miss de Vine.

> *'But you say you don't despise those who make some other persons their job?'*
>
> *'Far from despising them,' said Miss de Vine, 'I think they are dangerous.'*[1]

When Sayers was writing her novels eighty years ago, there was no doubt that a woman was to make her husband her 'full time job'. But it could only be described as a job to the extent that she gave him her undivided time and attention. She couldn't go blundering around and making mistakes about what was necessary to his happiness because she had failed to pay him enough attention. She had to be devoted. But this time, attention and devotion was not a job that she was ever going to be paid for. Well, she would be 'kept' and she would get the housekeeping money which was exactly what it said on the tin; if she wanted new clothes or a new couch, she had to ask him for more money. She was never paid a wage. Not by him and not by the state even though she was forewoman of the plant that the sociologists were now calling the basic unit of society.

But then nobody, not even the worker herself, thought she should get paid. She lived inside the contradiction that housework was not work. What married women did every day was not work—it was who they were, someone's wife and someone's mother. This is precisely how you lose your identity as Sheila. You lose your sense of self and become subsumed into these two roles. They take up all your time and all your energy and you never have enough of either left over to take responsibility for your self and the development of your own talents. If you do not think that it matters that this has happened to you then certainly nobody else does.

Throughout the years of her development every female child is formed by the common script of how to be wife and mother. Harriet or Sheila, or whoever she may be, the identity of each of these individuals is literally in mortal danger. As we saw in the previous chapter, over half a century since Sayers had stopped writing about Harriet and Peter, Susan Moller Okin was still outlining the stages of women's path to loss of independence. From beginning to end it is a case of *her* children and *his* job. Of course, at one level you were still Harriet or Sheila but the hard evidence witnesses to the fact that

---

1. *Gaudy Night*, 213.

you, the person, that individual site of goals, needs and desires, had disappeared. In your place a role emerged: You were now the good wife. And the definition of a good wife is someone whose primary job is to be a facilitating environment for her husband and family.

It is in this sense that Sayers refers to the fate of being devoured. To devour or be devoured is to take in or be taken in, ingested. Individuality is lost, identity is subsumed. See how it works: Mary Jones gets gobbled up and is regurgitated as Mrs. John Smith. Sayers acknowledges that it is possible for this to happen to either sex—men too can be devoured—but we know that it is mostly women who lose all sense of themselves as they follow the stereotypical gender roles that our culture has assigned to them.

Men have been given gender roles too. For this reason, it is not necessarily the individual husband that does the devouring but societie's expectations of what a good wife should be. Either way, many women lose confidence and ambition and, as they do, they hand over to their husbands the responsibility for being self-sufficient and productive members of their communities. This is a burden he proudly picks up as he lives out his assigned gender role as protector and provider. At which point we could, like Miss de Vine, feel sorry for the husband, the person who has become someone else's job. Because no matter how much he enjoys the time, the attention and the devotion, it does, as Sayers points out, have a devastating effect on his character. Many men lack confidence and ambition within the private sphere of the home. They too are under-developed and never achieve their full, human potential. They die in their droves from heart attacks because they cannot admit to vulnerability and find it hard to express their emotions.

But that is all in the past, isn't it? Today, wives and husbands are partners, equally sharing and caring for each other.

What happens today is that many young women enter the work force. They buy their own cars and maybe even their own homes. With financial independence comes a concomitant degree of self-determination. Some of them will even have secured a tertiary education first and with it the advantage of an even greater income. Nonetheless, it seems that all the while they are on the look out for a husband. They call off dates with girlfriends if 'he' calls. They diet relentlessly and increasing numbers, as we will see in the next chapter, even have plastic surgery. Botox is big and getting bigger. A different body as well as a different name.

No matter how much things have changed, no matter what the gains made by feminism, the fact remains that he has to be a success—read status or money or both—and she has to get a man. The implicit bargain, still, is that he will protect and provide and she will take care of the children. She might return to work after having the children, even between each birth, but her progress at work will slow down or stall. His job will then become primary and as a result she will have to be the first one to take time off if children or grandparents are ill. Like every other situation in life there are exceptions to this pattern but they are few and far between. Almost without exception, he would rather pay for a child minder and a house keeper than take time out from his job. His boss would definitely prefer that he did so.

All those years ago, Sayers was writing, not without hope: 'there are a few rare people, I believe, who don't look on themselves as jobs but as fellow creatures'. But, the numbers of equal couples are still rare, and for the others the situation is, as she says, dangerous. Dangerous might sound like too strong a word but it is unfortunately all too apt. When you lose your sense of identity you lose your voice. When you lose your voice, you are like a child: you can be seen but not heard. The old saying supposedly was directed at children but it really meant women too. In the world where women lose their sense of identity 'womenandchildren' really is one word.

'What's in a name?' they ask. 'Why, your whole self', is the reply.

Bless you, may your shadow never grow bulkier!

Strong Poison

Wimsey considered, rightly, that when a woman takes a man's advice about the purchase of clothes, it is a sign that she is not indifferent to his opinion.

Have His Carcase

Chapter 7
Vile Bodies

Rubens would not for a moment have considered painting the fashion model, Twiggy. The voluptuous form that he found so attractive, and helped to make so fashionable in the early seventeenth century, was considered gross in the twentieth. Twiggy was well named, she was a stick person. Form and fashion have changed over the centuries, from fat to thin and back again, over and over. Today, fat and fashion are feminist issues.

What shape we think a woman's body should be, and how she should clothe it, goes deep, almost into the unconscious. For many years now I had been used to considering myself a feminist with a thoroughly raised consciousness. Then, one day, I was walking along the beautiful beach in Derrynane, County Kerry in the south west of Ireland with my friend, Christine. A woman, with white skin, freckles and fat tummy, came walking towards us. According to conventional wisdom she was 'decidedly overweight'. She was wearing a bikini. 'How can she do that?' I said. It was a critical comment, not a question at all. Minutes later a man and two young boys came jogging towards us. He had a big, fat, beer belly hanging over his little blue Speedos. I kept on, walking and talking with Christine, with never a comment. A few minutes later, I stopped in my tracks. 'Do you realise what just happened? I was critical of that women's figure and he got past me unscathed!

Decidedly overweight. What does that mean, over what weight? Somebody, somewhere is setting a standard. The medics call it obesity. They will tell us that when we get to that point the weight is bad for our hearts, makes us prone to diabetes, puts stress on our joints and is generally contrary to good health. This applies, of course, to both men and women. All that is correct but although the question of weight might end with health issues it is definitely not where the problem begins.

Paradoxically, most of us who are labeled as having weight problems are perfectly healthy. Our so-called weight problems are not in the category of obesity but in the category of body image. The problem resides in our mind not in our body. Even painfully thin anorexics look in the mirror and see fat. The problem begins when the terms 'fat' and 'thin' no longer belong within the range of medical diagnosis, when we are neither obese nor anorexic, but when the words become pejorative and control our psychological health. Instead of fat being fat and thin being thin we have definitely decided at this time and in this place that fat is bad and thin is good - unlike Rubens. That is why clothes sizes for fat people are called 'plus' or 'extra' or 'outsize'—all words that fit into the over part of the word overweight. Sizes in single digits are not called 'minus' or 'less' or 'undersize' because these sizes do not need any further explanation. They are apparently the norm and the ideal. Thin is normal and large sizes represent the despised deviation.

The dictionary defines overweight as 'over a normal, desirable, permitted weight'. The first question that springs to mind on reading such a definition is who decides what is normal and permissable? In this context do 'normal' and 'desirable' contradict each other? Television, film, magazines and the entire fashion industry dictate the cultural ideal by giving us nothing but anorexic looking models. This is supposedly both normal and desirable.

Is the standard the same for both sexes? No, it is not. Men are allowed, even praised, for being overweight. These men are described as beefy, brawny and burly which means they are big and strong, nice positive terms but only when applied to males. The further women get away from being petite and dainty the more unattractive they become to themselves, to other women and apparently to men.

Today men are telling women all the time that they are too heavy. I have countless stories from my private practice as a psychotherapist. To their wives they say, 'No, don't wear that, it makes you look fat' or just straight out, 'You need to go on a diet'. Sometimes it comes as part of a string of abuse: 'you are stupid and lazy and fat'. To their daughters they say, 'Do you really need that?' as she reaches for dessert, or 'you should take more exercise, it'd be good for that bum if nothing else'. Men want their women to conform to this arbitrary standard of normal weight as much as the women themselves. And, as long as women will say 'I hate my fat thighs' or 'I am embarrassed by the size of my breasts' she threatens both femaleness and feminism.

Now any of these statements could have been made by women to men but they aren't. We are not surprised that Sayers puts the words, 'May your shadow never grow bulkier' into the mouth of Peter Wimsey. It is men who have always expressed the hope that women, their woman in particular, will not get fat. Susan Bordo lays it out in her book, *Unbearable Weight*: 'female hunger—for public power, for independence, for sexual gratification—[must] be contained, and the public space that women be allowed to take up be circumscribed, limited . . .'[1]

One generation of women after another go on diets all the time, they are never off them, and all you have to do is to open one of those fashion magazines or watch a Hollywood movie to understand why. It is estimated that more than 20% of women in the industrialised west are on a *constant* diet. Goodness only knows how many women are on multiple diets throughout their life time. An even more shocking statistic was produced by a MORI survey in Britain in January 2002: It was found that two thirds of young women would gladly give up their bodies for someone else's! Two thirds! That is a lot of self-disgust. And how many of the remaining third have some degree of disgust for their own bodies? Rich nations, we have a problem.

For myself, I would actually be embarrassed to list the number of weird and wonderful diets that I have embarked upon since the birth of my first child at the age of thirty-two. In the first place if I, and all the rest of dieting womanhood, embark on one diet after another, why did the penny not drop early in the process that they were not working? But these two pieces of information about myself are not unimportant because child birth and age are both extremely salient factors in the ways in which a woman's body changes and adapts. Women work hard to get their bodies 'back in shape' after childbirth and many of them succeed. But it *is* 'work' to conform once again

---

1. Susan Bordo, *Unbearable Weight* (Los Angeles: University of California Press, 1993), 171.

to the desirable and permitted shape. Hips get wider and breasts get bigger.

Women in the industrialised west are obsessed with their weight. Very few of us are content with our body shape to the extent that we never give it a thought, never step on a scales, never turn sideways in front of the mirror. It is a long time since the Duke of Cumberland wore a corset but women are still buying tens of thousands of them annually. Women that are the correct weight are intent on maintaining it. Women who are not are intent on achieving it. In both instances the mental pattern is the same: they think about their weight every day. Everything that goes into the mouth is monitored, and sometimes even by those who live with us. How often have you heard a woman say, I look ghastly, I really must put on some weight. May our shadows never grow bulkier is our constant and fervent daily prayer and hourly project.

Beyond the anxiety produced at the daily count of pounds or kilos, calories and kilojules, we have moved on, whipped into line by the advertising media, to the anguish of cosmetic procedures. There is no question that plastic surgery is a great gift in so many cases. When people have been burnt by house fires or had their jaw blown away by a bomb fragment it is nothing short of a miracle. Reconstructive surgery after breast cancer can bring comfort and relief. At the same time, we also think that societies that prescribe foot-binding or cliterodectomies are barbaric. But what about this for a little gem of western decadence: The American Society for Aesthetic Plastic Surgery reports that more and more of us are remaking our appearances every year. The year 2004 saw an increase of forty-four percent in the number of cosmetic procedures over 2003, including a record 2.8 million Botox injections, 1.1 million chemical peels, and hundreds of thousands of breast augmentations, eyelid surgeries, nose reshapings and liposuctions.[2] What the statistics do not include is a breakdown of how many of these operations were performed on women. And it is not that the patients report feeling anguish after the procedures—most of them are delighted with their new look—rather it is the anguish they suffer that makes them think they need to have

---

2. American Society for Aesthetic Plastic Surgery. (2004). Cosmetic Surgery. Quick facts: 2004 ASAPS statistics. Retrieved 16.11.2005 from http://www.surgery.org/press/statistics-2004.php.

these operations at all. This Society was only formed in 1931, and spent years reading learned papers to each other, at a time when Sayers was writing and women were treating their faces with the gentler and less expensive remedies of crushed strawberries, cucumber and mud.

The make-over of the body image has become even more intrusive, perhaps even sadder and certainly more dangerous. Today, we have arrived in the world of Designer Vaginas: labial reduction, vaginoplasty and hoodectomy. As with all forms of plastic surgery these operations can be performed for reasons of repair or discomfort. However, the doyens of the medical profession are both sceptical and critical. The American College of Obstetricians and Gynecologists says that they are not 'accepted and routine'.[3] In May, 2007, an article in the British Medical Journal blasted the 'vagina designer' craze because the rise in numbers was not produced by medical necessity but was rooted in commercial, pornographic and media influences. The Royal Australian and New Zealand College of Obstetricians and Gynecologists blacklisted the operations for exploiting vulnerable women not only to the tune of $10,000 but also by playing on insecurities and fears that would, they felt, be better dealt with by a psychologist. Like their colleagues from the northern hemisphere, they stated that these procedures had the potential to cause serious harm, often requiring reconstructive surgery.

I suppose if genitals are as different as faces, a bit of foresight could have predicted this sorry trend; why stop at the face? Perhaps the only good thing we can say about all this is that finally we have reached the end of the line. With nips, tucks, jabs, fat vacuuming and gastric banding already old hat, and toes shortened to fit into the latest designer shoes, women must finally have run out of bits of themselves to fix.

The bad news is that looking to a new wardrobe to boost your self-esteem or your sex life is a never ending, cyclical demand; the fashionable image changes from year to year and will cost a lot more than $10,000 in a life time. Women are taught from the outset to see themselves as the perfect candidates who will compete for male approval with their ideal physical type and their smart clothes. The clear message is that her body is not satisfactory as it is. It must be molded, it must be thin and free of unwanted hair, it must be

---

3. Http://archives.chicagotribune.com/2007/aug/31/news.

perfumed and, finally, it must be clothed in the height of annually changing fashions.

In the early 1930s, when Sayers was writing, the most daring of women had started to wear backless evening gowns to show off their suntans and tailored slacks in the style of Marlene Dietrich. My mother had such a pair and the Methodist minister, staying at the same resort, would not play croquet with her when they were drawn together in a competition. From slacks to bikinis in one generation is a big jump but we have to remember that what caused excitement one year was already dull by the next. This frantic activity goes hand in hand with Sayers suggestion 'that when a woman takes a man's advice about the purchase of clothes, it is a sign that she is not indifferent to his opinion'. She could have gone further and said that most women dress to gain a man's approval. What she is wearing and what shape is the body she is clothing requires constant obeisance before this other two-headed god that rules the lives of women. And this god is definitely a male god.

As we have seen, at an increasingly early age young women fall victim to the diet industry that sets up a standard for a body image that is impossible to meet. And then they have to keep competing with each other over clothes, and handbags, and shoes, and jewelry. In fact, the whole project becomes impossible as they twist this way and that to be sexy and nurturing, domestic goddesses and successful career women. It is no wonder that women suffer from depression; it is impossible, exhausting and expensive.

There is hope, however, as signs of common sense emerge. Second hand clothes can be acquired from Craigslist or Ebay. I know women who get together every year to exchange clothes. Fundraisers get their friends to donate clothes that can be sold to other friends. And what about crocs? Plastic clogs that are so comfortable that nurses, gardeners and the sane wear them all day.

But most of all we need to arrive at a place where we are not obsessed with the size of our shadows. Even more importantly, we need to return to the realisation that there is no harm in our shadows growing bulkier because big is also beautiful.

L'amour! These ladies come and dance and excite themselves and want love and think it is happiness. And they tell me about their sorrows—me—and they have no sorrows at all, only that they are silly and selfish and lazy. Their husbands are unfaithful and their lovers run away and what do they say? Do they say, I have two hands, two feet, all my faculties, I will make a life for myself? No. They say, Give me cocaine, give me the cocktail, give me the thrill, give me my gigolo, give me l'amo-o-ur! Like a mouton bleating in a field. If they knew!

Have His Carcase

I hope they'll be good girls, madam, and good wives and mothers—and that's what I'll bring them up to be.'

'I want to ride a motor-cycle when I'm bigger,' said Beatrice, shaking her curls assertively.

'Oh, no darling. What things they say, don't they, madam?'

'Yes, I do,' said Beatrice. 'I'm going to have a motor-cycle and keep a garage.'

'Nonsense,' said her mother, a little sharply. 'You mustn't talk so. That's a boy's job.'

'But lots of girls do boys' jobs nowadays,' said Harriet.

'But they ought not, madam. It isn't fair. The boys have hard enough work to get jobs of their own. Please don't put such things into her head madam. You'll never get a husband, Beatrice, if you mess about in a garage, getting all ugly and dirty.'

'I don't want one,' said Beatrice firmly. 'I'd rather have a motor-cycle.'

Annie looked annoyed; but laughed when Harriet laughed.

'She'll find out someday, won't she, madam?'

'Very likely she will,' said Harriet

Gaudy Night

Chapter 8
Dependency: Great Expectations

It is my belief that a great deal of the dependent condition experienced by most women is due to the fact that nobody ever expected them to be independent.

When boys are born, people ask, 'I wonder what he will do when he grows up?' Tinker, tailor, soldier, sailor? When a girl is born, nobody asks that question. It is not important that she have a career because her identity will not depend upon her income. Her end point is obvious because it is naturally predetermined: her function is reproduction; her identity is wife and mother. Of course, she cannot reproduce without a man but at a certain point along the way men seem to forget that, leaving their participation in reproduction conveniently short. She is going to marry and have children. All her life she is told that this is where happiness lies. From books and films, from her contemporaries, previous generations and parents, she learns that it is the happy marriage that makes a happy life. It does not matter what else she does, if she marries and has children, this is perceived by her and by everyone around her to be the fullness of life. It will be enough. Men too want a happy marriage but this private world will never be enough, it will not be the fullness of life for them. They must have a public profile. They must be independent.

It is a fact that, at least in what we know as the developed world, girls are educated to the same level as boys. But this fact of equal ability rarely produces equal expectations. I know young women who, even today, will tell me that lots of girls do a B.A. at university while they wait to get married. Female medical students opt for specialties that will give them more flexibility than surgery. Whatever employment option they pursue they even find it hard to take themselves seriously. They know, deep down, that as a mother they will spend a great deal more time with their children than will the father. It is not so much that they are 'silly, selfish and lazy' but many of them never really come to terms with the idea that, just like the boys, they too can say, 'I have two hands, two feet and all my faculties, I will make a life for myself!' With a third level degree they can teach, or get a corporate job, or work in a government department. But they do not plan this as the end point of their lives. What they are doing is marking time until Mr Right comes along. As one of my friends put it to me, 'we don't really take responsibility for ourselves'. Which is another way of saying that we do not hold great expectations for ourselves.

Failing to take responsibility for yourself presupposes a belief that someone else will step in to fulfill that role. Enter man, with prospects. Who, by the way, is usually taller and older and perceived to be smarter, at least by himself if not also by her. Mostly, women marry up and men marry down. Women are brainwashed to believe that if they do not get a man they can never be happy. I do not think I have ever heard a young woman say, I have chosen the single life and I love it. I have often heard young men say, I don't really need to get married. You only have to hear those Stags or Bucks Night stories to know that men regret the loss of what they believe is freedom. Women, who are going to have a Hens night party because they are going to lay the eggs and hatch them, are desperate to put on a ring.

It is a basic tenet of the conventional wisdom that spinsters are lonely, pathetic creatures, who sit in nights watching TV in their slippers. Once upon a time, bachelors, like squires, were young men aspiring to knighthood. Today they are still romantic creatures, interesting, public figures, socially much sought after and regularly invited to dinner parties. To lead a bachelor's existence is to lead a life. Spinsters are life-less goods that have been 'left on the shelf'. A single woman, an unmarried woman, as described by the lawyers, is a *femme sol*: a woman without a man. Sad, incomplete thing. Men are never defined in this way, they are simply and completely, men. They are subject to no legal description that is defined by their marital status. Happy, consummate individual.

But even worse than feeling sorry for herself in her uncoupled state, it is even more excruciating to know that everyone else feels sorry for her too. Alone, she must always be unfulfilled. The shame of being a wall flower is little short of excoriating. What convinces me of the truth of this is the number of middle-aged women I have met who dread widowhood or being divorced because of the ensuing isolation. Men provide women entry into the world which is still a man's world. They confer status upon her. She might walk into a party alone but she does not like doing it. Her social standing is derivative, from her father and then from her husband. Left alone a woman tends to disappear.

Furthermore, only women can be 'left on the shelf' or 'wall flowers'. In Sayers' day, it was the women who had to make sure that their bodies were in the right shape and that they were wearing the latest fashion, faces painted, hair done. They had to be attractive. Only then were they ready to line up against the wall while the men stood on the other side of the room, eyeing them all, contemplating their selection.

If a young man was without a partner because he was shy, that was an individual, personality problem. He was still a member of the powerful caste. If you were a woman and were not asked to dance, you had no choice but to sit. Imagine a woman crossing the floor to ask one of the men to dance. Women were not allowed to choose their men, to be the selectors rather than the selectees. Men acted, women were acted upon. One assertive, the other passive. The only difference between then and now is that today most of the dancers will end up in bed with each other. But, never doubt it, the same theme is still there, running beneath all their interactions. While on any given Saturday night he is looking for sex, she is looking for a life partner who will give her status and security. And, when she finds him, she will not be the one to propose.

Feminism has made a substantial difference to the lives of both women and men. We live in a brave new world where women can vote for women candidates and a female judge can pass sentence on a man and send him to prison. Where once she was air hostess she is now pilot; instead of nurse she is now doctor. As Harriet observed, 'lots of girls do boys' jobs nowadays'.

What can we make of this observation, that women have entered the world of men, ostensibly as equals, doing men's work and sometimes even earning men's pay?

Women's entry into public life is undoubtedly very important, not least because it provides them with financial independence. And the more your bank balance increases the better you feel about yourself and the more respect you generate in the opposite sex. We know that the main reason for female dependency is that women have always been financially dependent and the man's world was organised to keep it that way. But leaving aside structural oppression and its glass ceiling for the moment—we will return to that in a later chapter—let us suppose that everyone around you expected you to be successful, or at least self-sufficient. The subject of great expectations, you would blossom into independence. You might, like Beatrice, proclaim that instead of a husband you would like to ride a motor bike and own a garage, both the symbol and the fact of masculinity.

By independence, I mean independence of a psychological variety. This form of independence involves loving yourself in such a way that you are actually content to be single even if *l'amour* and a life partner is your first choice. It is the kind of independent contentment that understands that being alone is very different from being lonely.

Given what we have already discovered about being a spinster this is not at all an easy choice to make for an individual woman. A single man is admired and sought after; a single woman is an object of pity. You are going to have to think about yourself in a very different way, to take responsibility for yourself and your life, in fact, to have expectations of yourself. You are going to have to stand up for yourself in the face of deeply ingrained cultural perceptions. Only then can you pursue your own particular talent or vocation, to become the best possible you, with little or no thought as to whether you might meet Mr Right along the way.

These are not choices that women still, today, find it easy to make because whatever gains feminism has made we still live in a world where she must get a man and he must be successful. To be single-minded in pursuit of your own career is seen to be threatening in a woman while it is considered admirable, even essential, in a man. He is doing what he is supposed to be doing, what his masculinity requires; she has crossed over, endangered her femininity, challenged men at their own game.

But, pause . . . what if men gave up on the idea of competition with each other and decided that being in right relation with another person in terms of *l'amour* and care-giving was better than independence and, in fact, the only way to become their best possible selves? Admittedly, this would be no easy task for a man, to have as his other primary goal in life being a continually facilitating environment for those he professes to love, but a fascinating prospect to contemplate. In fact it is, I have met some. Nonetheless, it seems plausible to conclude that he would find it just as difficult as she does to change the way he thinks about himself. It is not easy to change our deep seated beliefs about gender roles. As Annie said of her daughter, Beatrice, 'she'll find out someday . . .' just how hard it is to undermine the bulwarks of gender stereotypes.

But in turning themselves inside out each sex would now discover what had been pushed down, lying dormant, hidden even from themselves. What they would bring into the light was that part of themselves that had been forbidden by the culture, by the message that said 'men are born this way' and 'women are born that way'.

Now they would be in a position to teach each other what they had learned from this half-human construction of themselves, these deformed identities of masculinity and femininity that represented only half of the humanity with which they were really born. From him she could learn the values of independence and self-reliance and how to take responsibility for developing her talents, beyond those of wife and mother. From her he could learn a widely expanded set of emotional responses that allowed him to be both dependent and autonomous, an affective and attentive carer for those around him. They would begin to approach the possibility of full humanity as they learned to be *inter*dependent.

A good marriage must be predicated on interdependence. We have seen that to have one sex dependent upon the other precludes the possibility of equality. We do not want the sexes to trade places because dependence can never be a one way street. Women and men are both dependent upon each other because they are relational beings. Both of them need to share responsibility for both the home and the workplace, for their children and their livelihood. This joint, shared responsibility can be summed up in that one word: interdependence.

Quite simply, women already know that to be only feminine is to be only half human. This is why they started the feminist movement. It is for men to recognise now that to be only masculine is to be only half human. If both sexes start from a recognition that the opposite sex has always held their other half in trust for them then to depend upon the other is no more than a homecoming, a coming home to the full self. As we appreciate that we are not only relational beings but also interdependent ones, we can construct a moral theory that accommodates individual autonomy and human relationships better. We see all human beings, their interests, their moral potential, all that they are capable of, as essentially related and interdependent. Now that we have all the pieces of the puzzle we must assemble them in the race to be human.

Men cannot be forced to give up the power they currently hold over women but if they do not they need to admit that their choice is irrational. Just as they have denied their dependence upon nature any continuation of their denial of dependency upon women will end in disaster. The jury is still out on whether men, as a class, believe that women are their equal.

. . . When she saw herself in the glass, she laughed. 'An arum-lily quality that is in itself an invitation to violence.' . . .

Poor Philip—tormented by his own vanities, never loving her till he had killed her feelings for him . . .

Gaudy Night

Chapter 9
Violence!

Being hit is terrifying. Being punched, knocked down and kicked until your ribs break and your skull cracks is enough to make a grown man weep. Men know the fear of violence and knowing it, they know how to use it as a weapon, as the saying goes, in love and war.

But all is not fair in love and war when men use violence against women. Men are stronger than women so the two are never equally matched. We have all seen pictures of a man, holding a young boy at arms length while the youngster flails with both fists but can never connect. A bantam weight is never put in the ring with a heavy weight. Men know the rules but when they get angry with women, far too often they do not keep them.

I still find it amazing that men will say to me when we are doing couples therapy together, 'She hit me first, you know', as if somehow it should now be clear to me that they are both equally responsible for the violence that has occurred between them. When a woman pushes or slaps a man it might be shocking to him, it might annoy or anger him, or all of the above. What it does not do is terrify him. In fact, when she slaps or pushes him, or even bites him or spits at him— women do not use close fists—she is probably now more frightened that him. The thought that immediately occurs is 'now he is going to be really angry'.

Women can, and do, commit violent acts against men. Even to the point of murder. But if she is going to injure him while he is awake, she will probably have to do it from a distance. Let us say with a gun, a sort of David and Goliath. If he is asleep, she could stick a knife between his ribs, or hit him with that baseball bat, or set the house on fire. But it is undeniable that when he is awake and they are within arms reach of each other, he is safe and she is vulnerable. Even if she wants to hit him, he can hold her arms by her sides. If he wants to hit her there is nothing she can do to stop him. We do not hear about women locking him into the bedroom or taking his car keys to keep him in the house so she can do what she wants to him. One of my female clients had both of her arms broken. I never had a male client, or heard of one, who had both of his arms broken by his wife. Women simply do not scare men, not physically.

Men absolutely terrify women and to be a victim of physical violence you have to be frightened. Now each time you are frightened does not always mean that you have been hit. A man can control a woman for years without ever touching her; he simply uses the memory of violence. If he hits her once then every time she sees that clenched fist or that look on his face, or that belt wrapped around his knuckles, she knows that it might happen again. Some women say his eyes narrow, others that his eyes widen. Some say his lips are pulled back in a snarl, others that his lips become thin. Still others say that he will go very quiet and start drumming his fingers on the table. Whatever form the memory takes, she already has proof that he is capable of hitting her. It really does not matter that he can say, 'Well, yes, I did hit her once but it was only once and that happened fifteen years ago'. It is the memory alone that is sufficient to control her.

Even the law recognises this as violent behaviour. Law makes the distinction between assault and battery. For an assault to take place there need be no physical contact at all. It is sufficient that the victim has reasonable cause to believe that he can do what he is threatening to do so that she is 'put in fear'. Battery means battery, it means connecting.

One of the most frightening things about violence is the frequency with which it happens. There is really no way to assess the amount of times that an assault takes place because when battery is absent the attack is almost never reported. In fact most women still believe that no domestic violence has taken place if she has not been hit. Likewise the statistics on battery are incomplete due to under-reporting. We can only shiver at how horrifying the situation is in reality when we are confronted with the facts that we do have.

Violence against women is a global pandemic of alarming proportions according to the United Nations. The statistics are numbing when we realise that across the globe, six out of every ten women experience physical or sexual violence in their lifetime.[1] We were most recently reminded of these figures by the One Billion Rising, a world-wide campaign initiated and organised by Eve Ensler (author of the *Vagina Monologues*)[2] which took place on 14 February 2013.

In 1994 a World Bank study on ten selected risk factors facing women and girls in the age group sixteen to forty-four years, found rape and domestic violence more dangerous than cancer, motor vehicle accidents, war and malaria. This makes the physical and sexual violence to which women are submitted the most pervasive human rights violation we know today.

Sexual violence around the world takes many forms. The United Nations estimates that there are one hundred and thirty million women alive today who have been subjected to Female Genital Mutilation and that a further two million girl children are at risk every year. And do not be fooled, this violence is not confined to places that many of us could not locate on the map. It continues among immigrant populations around the globe, from Australia to Britain where doctors can be faced with nothing but a wall of scar tissue.

'Honour Killings' occur when a man feels a woman has dishonoured him or his family. Here the United Nations estimates the figure might be as high as five thousand—every year.

In India in 2002, it is known that 6,822 women died as a result of Dowry Murder. There were undoubtedly many more unreported and unnamed victims.

Early marriage is a common practice to re-fund the family. In Afghanistan the United Nations estimates that fifty-seven per cent of girls are 'sold' into marriage before they reach sixteen years. This girl child-asset may be cashed in as early as six years of age with the agreement that the marriage be delayed until puberty. This is an

---

1. Http://www.unifem.org/gender_issues/violence_against_women/ and the UNITE to End Violence Against Women Campaign, 2008, initiated by the UN Secretary-General's Office.
2. See www.onebillionrising.org

agreement that is rarely observed and the girl is frequently raped by older men in the family, especially where the groom is also a child.

It is this form of violence, what we sickeningly call domestic violence, that is either physical or sexual and takes place within the home, within the family or within an intimate relationship. In no country in the world are women safe from this kind of violence. The United Nations reports state that the incidence reaches a staggering seventy-one percent in rural Ethiopia but in western, industrialised nations the figures are also shocking: thirty percent in the United Kingdom, twenty-two per cent in the United States. In Australia nearly a quarter of women who have been married, or lived in a *de facto* relationship, have experienced violence by their partner.[3] In Ireland a national study found that forty-two percent of girls and women experienced sexual violence in their lifetime, 20.4% as adults. With respect to physical violence in a domestic setting, 8,452 incidents were reported to the police. Only 1,418 led to an arrest and a paltry 650 (seven percent) resulted in a conviction.[4]

What we rarely think of as domestic violence is the form of abuse to which Sayers refers. She writes of her heroine, Harriet and her lover: 'Poor Philip—tormented by his vanities, never loving her till he had killed her feelings for him'. He wanted to believe that he was a better writer than she, that there was more substance to the subject matter of his books, that she should have been at the service of his talent. There are so many Philips who engage in this silent killer of love and affection. It is called emotional abuse.

Of course emotional abuse can be practiced by either sex. That being the case, it is quite likely the most common form of abuse. She can, for example, taunt him with the fact that he is too stupid or too lazy to ever succeed at anything. We have several studies that provide data to the effect that women also engage in domestic violence towards the men they live with. And some men are badly affected by the emotional abuse to which they are subjected. Nonetheless, just as women and men do not come equally to other relationships,

---

3.   Http://www.aic.gov.au/en/media2000. Press Release, Senator Amanda Vanstone, Minister for Justice and Customs. April 6th, 2000.

4.   McGee *et al.* and the Dublin Rape Crisis Centre. SAVI (Sexual Abuse in Ireland) *A National Study of Irish Experiences, Beliefs and Attitudes concerning Sexual Violence*. (Dublin: Liffey Press, 2002).

they do not come to this type of abusive relationship with the same degree of power and the same options. Even mild-mannered and well behaved men who are affected by emotional abuse are still mostly in a position of superior power. It is not that women do not earn their own money, some even have substantial incomes, and a few have even been known to leave their children. Almost invariably, however, he carries a heavier wallet and a lighter sense of responsibility for the children both of which leave him with a greater degree of freedom to walk out of the home and leave her to mind them.

Just as he has more power, so too he has more options when both parties are engaging in emotional abuse. The real problem for her is that, unlike him, she has no fall back position, no Plan B. If she engages in the emotional abuse of her partner, she runs a real risk. The most frightening statistic is the one we have already discussed: that men beat women and they hurt them badly, sometimes even to death. If she taunts him too well how much more likely is he to turn to violence to shut her up? If he chooses to move on from verbal and emotional abuse to physical and sexual harm we know that he can and that is a game he will win. If a woman wants to engage in the emotional abuse of her husband, she should have the front door open, the keys in her hand and the engine running.

Year in and year out, women put up with being put down: Fat, stupid, hysterical, nuts, whore, frigid. They let him have control of the family money: 'You had better come in here right now and tell me what is all this stuff on the credit card'. They have sex when they do not want to and take the pill for years so they will be available when he does want to. All in all, both of them seem to agree that his needs are greater than hers. At the very least, she spends a great deal more time trying to meet his needs than he does hers.

Violence can be noisy and it can be a silent look, it can be in the wound or in the threat, it can cause a bruise or it can cause palpitations. It often causes miscarriages. Whatever form it takes, it is always unacceptable. When a man provides an explanation for why he hit a woman, he must come to see that it is just that—an explanation, because it can never be an excuse. There is no excuse for violence, it is not an acceptable option no matter how angry he feels. Listen carefully when a man says, 'I just saw red', or 'I was out of control, I couldn't help myself' because in these circumstances he will very carefully control where he lands the punch. It will be somewhere that cannot be detected. Listen carefully too when a man apologises with the words, 'I am really sorry that it happened'. He needs to understand that 'it' did not just happen—he did it, and for this he is responsible.

We know that men were hitting women when Sayers was writing, just as they are today. We know that women are putting up with more violence than they should, either because they have no options or fear they have no options, or 'for the sake of the children'. We also know that as a society we are still not doing enough to protect women. Violence against women is global and it is systemic. It is part of the structures of a patriarchal world in which men dominate women. The Beijing Platform for Action (1995), reflects this when it states that 'violence against women is a manifestation of the historically unequal power relations between men and women, which have led to domination over and discrimination against women by men and to the prevention of women's full advancement'.

We need more men to speak out, like Eli Manning and the American football teams who produced a powerful advertisement condemning violence. We need them because there are not enough refuges and there are not enough places in the refuges that we do have. There are not enough police or social workers assigned specifically to deal with this problem, endemic within our societies. And there are not enough men taking responsibility for the continuous acts of physical, verbal and sexual assaults with the explicit aim of hurting, degrading, intimidating and silencing women by what is criminal and inhuman behaviour. These acts always violate the human rights of women. At the personal and intimate level it is the man who will lose not his life but what he needs in life. At the end of the day it is the man, just as Sayers wrote, who, like Philip Boyes, will never realise what he has lost until he has killed her love for him.

'At any rate, in March of 1928, the prisoner, worn out, as she tells us, by his unceasing importunities, gave in, and consented to live on terms of intimacy with him, outside the bonds of marriage.

Now you may feel, and quite properly, that this was a very wrong thing to do . . . . . . Sir Impey Biggs, very rightly using all of his great eloquence on behalf of his client . . . has reminded you that, in such a situation, the woman always has to pay more heavily than the man.

Philip Boyes and the prisoner lived together in this fashion . . . for nearly a year. Various friends have testified that they lived on terms of the greatest mutual affection. Miss Price said that, although Harriet Vane obviously felt her unfortunate position very acutely—cutting herself off from her family and friends and refusing to thrust herself into company where her social outlawry might cause embarrassment and so on—yet she was extremely loyal to her lover and expressed herself proud and happy to be his companion.'

Strong Poison

Chapter 10
The Sexual Double Standard

We are long past the day when a young woman, living with her boyfriend, would be cast as a social outlaw. Women have ready access to the pill and, if they are wise, condoms, and are now sleeping with whomever they want, whenever they want. So long, of course, as it is only with one person. Women are not allowed to have multiple partners, not simultaneously. 'Sleeping around' could still get her outlawed.

'Sleeping around' is a good place to begin when talking about the sexual double standard. We like to think that the sexual revolution has given every person equal access to sexual activity. Well, it has and it has not. On the one hand, although women can sleep with anyone they want, the consequences of such a choice remain different for each sex. She can still be called 'easy' or 'loose' while his good times are called getting experience, learning to become the good lover. The more sexual partners she attracts the more criticism she attracts; the more sexual partners he has the bigger the 'stud' he becomes. 'Boys will be boys' but society does not give women permission to sew their wild ova.

While all this promiscuous sexual activity is taking place, he is preparing for marriage and she is becoming increasingly less eligible. All these so-called studs want plenty of sex but none of them want to marry 'soiled goods'. Only last year, I heard one male doctor say of an unmarried female doctor who had become pregnant, 'She is going to find it hard to get a husband'. Well, if not hard, certainly harder. Men are not inclined to raise another man's child. Yet, how is it that nobody ever says, would ever think to say, that a male doctor who impregnates his girlfriend is going to find it harder to find a wife.

Social mores have undergone seismic shifts since Harriet Vane first fell in love. While her decision in 1928 to live with her lover was considered immoral by almost the entire population of the United Kingdom of Great Britain, today, in Ireland for example, cohabiting couples are the fastest growing form of family unit. In 1996 there were 31,000 couples living together, but ten years later the census of 2006 showed that there are now 121,800 such couples, which is to say, one in every twelve family units.[1] All across the developed world the drift is in the same direction. In the United States, cohabitation was first noted and researched as a cultural phenomenon in the 1970s, it exploded in the 1980s and between 1990 and 2000 the number of cohabiting couples increased by seventy-two percent.[2] Today, the number of couples living together is at an all time high, rising thirteen percent from 6.7 million in 2009 to 7.5 million in 2010 (US Census Bureau, 2010).

Even when a woman marries and has a child the sexual double standard lives on. A female friend of mine, married to a solicitor, was adamant that her husband was badly treated when a young, married, female solicitor that he hired had the nerve to get pregnant. After all, he had hired her to attend to his clients, not to take maternity leave. Of course, you can see their problem—he never took any time off to care for their two babies when they were born. He could not do that, he said, 'because lawyers offices just do not work that way, it would simply be chaotic if we walked out of the office at regular intervals to look after our kids'. The young, female lawyer is not allowed to get pregnant but when her husband does his employer will buy him a cigar. Which leads us back to the old double standard that is embedded in our attitudes to child care. Where leave to care for infants exists it is, as we saw in Chapter 4, mostly provided for women, inadequate but present. Which is not to say that fathers have been entirely left out. By 2016, Australia and New Zealand will rank twenty-sixth in the OECD (Organisation for Economic Co-operation and Development) by providing eighteen weeks of paid parental leave. Germany and Japan provide fifty-eight weeks. A shift in attitudes was bolstered by the 'Dad and Partner Pay' scheme in Australia which provided two weeks pay at minimum wage level but that is very little compared to

---

1. *Irish Independent*, 15 February 2011.
2. 'Cohabitation Statistics', *Family Life and Culture Watch*, 22 February 2008.

the situation in the UK where parents can split thirty seven weeks of paid parental leave.[3]

There is a lot hidden in the phrase, 'offices do not work this way'. At one level it is a true description of a current reality but there is no reason that this cannot change. Offices, or institutions or professions only work the way people want them to work. Take for example the field of medicine. Young women enter this profession in ever increasing numbers and as they graduate and start to work, male doctors begin to fret. The *British Medical Journal* worries that medical staffing is nearing a crisis, not just in Britain but also in Canada and the United States because there are more women than men entering the profession. In January, 2008, Macleans, a Canadian magazine, reported that fifty-two percent of Canadian doctors under thirty-five years of age were women and that by 2015 women would make up forty percent of the nation's total physician work force.[4]

This is a problem apparently. The explicit reason given for this problem is that the patient will suffer. A woman doctor is more likely to work part-time. It seems that women doctors want to reduce their work commitments and not work out of hours, or maybe they even want to quit altogether and not return until the children are grown. What seems like a sensible plan—to retire before they are sixty—is met with disapproval by male colleagues. Women doctors simply do not provide 'a life span of contributions' to the profession and to the patient.

The tacit reason for the problem, and arguably the real reason, is that his home and his family are going to suffer. These men will say—with a perfectly straight face—her family duties will detract from her professional contribution and her work-life will negatively impact on her domestic responsibilities. They are in no doubt, that even despite years of feminist discourse, women still have to double job. They must mind the home and take primary responsibility for the children, a pull, incidentally, that the husband and father apparently does not feel.

---

3. See 'Comment' in *Sydney Morning Herald* 6 June 2015. www.smh.com.au
4. Cathy Gulli and Kate Lunau, 'Adding Fuel to the Doctor Crisis', 2 January 2008. www.macleans.ca/health/science

Echoing that early, aspiring feminist, John Stuart Mill, the notion is still abroad that although a woman may certainly work and earn her own income, if she chooses to have a family then career must come second. If the woman doctor herself does not want to put her career in second place she is much more likely than her male counter part to suffer burnout, according to Dr Janet Dollin, president of the Federation of Medical Women of Canada. She states what we all know nearly off by heart at this point: 'Despite their demanding careers, women are still given the bigger proportion of child care, housekeeping and elder care'. The pressure drives many women out of medicine altogether.

In the current set up of medical life, just as in other areas of work-life, a woman finds it very hard to win. If she engages in part-time work, she is not making the same 'life span of contribution'. Yet, if she works full-time, she is neglecting her husband and family.

Men in the medical profession are not saying that a woman should not also be a doctor. But they are making it very difficult for her to work and raise her family. The reason is obvious: men, in this case male doctors, do not want to change the structure of their work lives so that they can share fully in home-making and child rearing. They never think of themselves as having to double job. Yet, these are the very men who themselves have homes and have children. The interesting point is, however, that when a woman works, for money, part-time and then goes home to the 'second shift' of housework and children, she will have worked, for money and for no money, more hours than her male counterpart who is working, for money, full-time and ostensibly making that so commendable 'life span of contribution'.

It is simplistic to blithely state that justice requires that the rules of the job must apply equally to both sexes. Which is to say, that if a woman wants to be treated equally in the profession then she must take on an equal work load. At first glance this seems an eminently reasonable position to maintain. However, when we look at the rule through the lens of a sexual double standard all we see is a persistent discrimination against women. For the simple reason that the rule applies to women at work but not to men at home.

However, equality is not beyond our reach, not if we really want it. If we really want it, and staying with our example of the medical model, let us start to treat doctors like pilots. Both groups have extremely responsible and stressful jobs. For this reason pilots are limited to 35hrs duty per week. That would be very sensible for doctors. Each one of them could reduce their hours so that they would be well rested and at their most effective when they were on duty. Reduced hours would mean that both sexes would have more time to attend to their children and their golf handicap. They would actually all have a life, a balanced one, albeit with a reduced income. But then money is not everything. Is it?

If we adopted this approach men would be adopting women's preferred work patterns. Because men also marry and have children it would be helpful for everyone, including the patients, if all doctors enjoyed more flexibility. They could enjoy the benefits of job sharing, part-time posts, sessional arrangements and retraining and re-entry programs for whichever parent opted to stay home with the children until they were raised. All in all, a program that is not too shocking and not too difficult to arrange. In fact, a program suggested by Mr. George McNeice, Chief Executive of the Irish Medical Association at their Annual General Meeting, 20 April 2001. And a course of action adopted by Hamot Medical Centre in Erie, Pa. that filled one obstetric post with a husband and a wife. They shared one salary and worked out their own schedules for home and hospital.

Just a word of caution. When we engage with the sexual double standard in relation to 'affairs', wives can engage in their own brand of double standard when it comes to his infidelity. I cannot tell you the number of female clients I have had who are absolutely adamant that the 'other woman' is immoral, disgusting, a home wrecker, a vampire, a shrew and always a slut. But not her husband. He cannot be anything unforgivable if she is going to have him back home after the affair. He is the poor fellow who has been led astray by this wicked woman. Even when I suggest to her that maybe when he met this other woman, he told her that his wife was a nag, had no time for him at all and that he was in one of the most unhappy marriages known to man. She likes him a lot, believes his sad sincerity and does not think she is doing anything to harm the wife because his wife clearly does not love him any more. The fact is, my client-wife is not able to require the same degree of accountability from her husband that she demands of the 'other woman'. The wife can never forgive her for breaking 'the bonds of marriage' while she is very ready to forgive her husband for breaking the same bonds.

Nonetheless, as Dorothy Sayers pointed out to us, 'the woman always has to pay more heavily than the man'. The bar is always set higher for women. When it comes to sexual morality, modest, pure and chaste are not attributes we commonly require of men yet the white wedding dress is loaded with symbolism. Even at work, a woman fire fighter, for example, must be better than a man if she wants to hold onto her job. And that is equally true on the shop floor, in politics or the boardroom. Which only goes to show that in the intervening eighty years since Sayers wrote these cautionary words, very little has changed. And they will not, until men decide that women, as human beings like themselves, are entitled to the same rights and privilege.

Catherine Freemantle, it seemed, had married a farmer and everything had gone wrong . . . working one's fingers to the bone and bringing up children. Harriet . . . felt she would rather be tried for life over again than walk the daily treadmill of Catherine's life.

'But Miss Freemantle—I mean, Mrs—Mrs. Bendick—it's absurd that you should have to do this kind of thing. I mean, pick your own fruit and get up at all hours to feed poultry and slave like a navvy. Surely to goodness it would have paid far better for you to take on some kind of writing or intellectual job and get someone else to do the manual work.'

'Yes, it would. But . . . my husband wouldn't have liked it much if I had separated myself from his interests.'

'What a damned waste! was all Harriet could say to herself.

Gaudy Night

Chapter 11
The Handmaiden: in the House

The tale of Catherine Freemantle is a cautionary one. Beware of educating yourself, getting a good job, enjoying all the benefits of financial independence, and then returning to the home to raise the children. Beware of taking your husband's name and of becoming totally absorbed in his interests. If you do, like Catherine Freemantle, you will live his life but lose your own.

Losing your life in the service of another is the fate of the handmaiden. We hear it in biblical terms, when Mary declared, 'Behold, the handmaid of the Lord', meaning I will give my life to serve you; you may dispose of me as you will. In the ancient world, handmaiden was also a common euphemism for concubine. Bileh was selected to bear a child for her master, Jacob. In modern literature, Margaret Atwood's *The Handmaid's Tale*, relates the story of a woman used as a concubine to assist sterile couples in an oppressive future society.

On the other hand, handmaidens might also be highly born, even royal, and as such, well educated companions to their mistresses, like the ladies-in-waiting to the Renaissance and Tudor Queens of France and England. A very old and very fine example is Miresaki Shikibu, attendant to the Japanese Empress Shoshi in the eleventh century. She was the author of the world's first novel, *The Tale of Genji*. She, at least, must have had a considerable amount of free time.

A handmaiden, like a lady-in-waiting, is always an attendant, an assistant or a servant. Whatever her education, even despite it, she is the helper, the one who enables someone else to lead their life. Even allowing for the level of comfort that comes with living in royal courts, these women enjoyed no freedom of movement to come and go as they pleased. They were also not free to speak their minds. Like Catherine Freemantle, they lacked a voice, simply because their masters or mistresses would not have been pleased if they had separated their interests from theirs.

There are two main categories of the handmaiden in the home. There is the wife who helps her husband to live his life and there is the domestic or cleaner who helps the wife who helps the husband. In both categories women pay a price to be a handmaiden.

The first group, the group of wives, can be roughly divided into three classes, the rich, the middle class and the poor. They all live in their own homes, largely of their own shaping and they are, to varying degrees, fed, warmed and clothed. While each of them pay a price to be provided for in this way, it is the middle class group that run the greatest risk in the greatest numbers. The wealthy can afford to divorce and be without the protection that marriage offers because there is always enough money for another house and a substantial settlement. Money buys options as well as the other necessities of a comfortable life. Those who are poor are familiar with economic hardship, and while never inured to it, the fact remains that if you do not own your own home, you cannot lose it. If the state is housing you married, it will house you single. There might be a waiting list for government housing but it is eventually available. 'Freedom', as the song says, 'is just another word for nothing left to lose'.

It is the middle class woman whose circumstances will be considerably altered post-divorce. She can leave her marriage but she will take a substantial drop in living standards for herself and her children. Most of this group live on their overdrafts already. They spend as they earn, consuming cars, TV's and holidays and endless extras for the children. They cannot afford private clinics and they earn too much for a medical card. Saving is often not possible and where it is, it is not fashionable. So, a drop in living standards is inevitable. Where there was enough money for one set of utility bills there is not enough for two. Dividing the already accounted for family pot results in everyone being dragged downwards.

The question that most women are asking themselves today is: is being a handmaiden still worth the cost? All women, whatever their economic circumstances are asking this question.

For the very well educated and wealthy women it appears that being a handmaiden is still, you might say, value for money. This might appear strange given that this is the group that enjoys the greatest choice and mobility. For example, in the United States in 1950, less than three quarters of college educated women were married by the age of forty, compared to ninety percent of their contemporaries who left formal education after completing high school.[1] If we projected directly from these figures to today's education data which shows us how many women are going to college, we would expect the marriage rate to have rapidly declined over the pasty sixty years. But this is not so. True, graduates marry later but they are reaping the benefits of the feminist movement: women do a bit less housework and men do a bit more. The same goes for child rearing participation. If these educated and financially secure women want to balance work, fun and family they can. Money buys home help. And, as I have already mentioned, whatever the gains of feminism, women still feel the cultural pressure to marry. It is not surprising then, that in this educated group we find marital happiness is higher and divorce rates have fallen sharply. On the down side, one obvious difficulty that looms is that if women keep outstripping men in graduate numbers, they are going to find that there is a shrinking pool of intellectual soul-mates to nest with.

At the other end of the economic scale, women with low incomes and without college education, women, that is, whose options and horizons are greatly limited form another substantial group of handmaidens. The cost of child care makes work outside the home, even if they could get it in these recessionary times, not a viable option.

Strangest of all, it appears to be the woman with the most to lose, the middle class woman, who is kicking hardest against the constraints of being a handmaiden in the house. It is this group that makes us least sanguine about the permanency of modern marriage. This is the group that is divorcing in the greatest numbers. This group has benefitted from third level education and many of these women have experienced satisfying, productive and lucrative jobs before returning to the home. They know first hand what financial independence, mobility and status feel like. But these very married

---

1. Betsy Stevenson, Wharton School, University of Pennsylvania, 'The Room Debate', in *The New York Times*, 21 February 2010.

women, with long years of service in the home and with children half grown, are initiating divorces. And with justification because not only are we not seeing any great rise in the numbers of stay-at-home dads, we are definitely not seeing many 50/50, 'I love and respect you, we are equals' dads. He does not want to be one of those handmaiden persons. Note: there is no male equivalent for the term.

The old feminist adage remains relevant: The greatest indicator of equality in a marriage is a woman's ability to insist on shared housework. Housework, as second wave feminism pointed out, is about power. More recently, Barbara Ehrenreich has echoed this argument, agreeing that housework is degrading, not because it involves manual labour but because it is embedded in degrading relationships.[2] Leaving wet towels on the bathroom floor or dirty dishes in the TV room is, believe it, the exercise of power. It might look like laziness or indifference and it certainly looks small and insignificant in the grand scheme of marriage but because she can keep asking him, please, not to do it and he can keep on doing it, regardless, it is an exercise in mastery and subordination. Which is a simple way of pointing out that there are very few equal marriages. So, what do you do, if mum is going to paid work and dad is definitely not into house work?

One strategy to ease the strain, that is suggested by Sayers and adopted by most mothers who are working full or part-time, is getting 'someone else to do the manual work' in the home. Because housework is woman's work it is the wife who will hire the help, supervise and sometimes even pay her. But whoever pays for the maid the home has now become a workplace. What feminism argued for in the early days—wages for housework—has now come to pass in the form of this paid handmaiden.

The context of the domestic worker has been described as the perfect storm where gender, race and class coincide. Amongst the rich and the middle-class this has become a nearly universal option. There are several problems with this solution. One of them is that young, mostly white children, learn that their needs will be met by mostly black or brown women. There are vast numbers of Filipino

2.   Barbara Ehrenreich, 'Maid to Order: The Politics of Other Women's Work', in *Harper's Magazine*, 1 April 2000.

women, from Hong Kong, to London to New York, who are working as housekeepers in the homes of the wealthy.

Another problem occurs at the level of public policy. So long as there is a pool of poor women to take care of the homes and the children of the wealthy there is no need for the state to consider, and make proper provision for, the structural changes that would have to be made if adequate child care was to be available. Which, of course, is something that only working women require. On the other hand, the independent house worker usually commands good hourly rates, usually in the region of US$15 to €15 per hour. Nonetheless, not too many maids would choose this work if they had something better to do with their time, like the woman who employs them; like me.

My husband and I, two able-bodied people, had someone who helped us for two hours every week with our housework. When our children lived at home, I would not let her into their bedrooms to clean until they had tidied them. At no level, however subtle or subliminal, did I want them to learn that they were more worthy than anyone else. In the same way, I pick up towels and 'straighten up' the hotel room I have just paid for before the maid arrives, and I always fold my blanket and pick up rubbish that I have dropped around my aircraft seat. The same applies to the train. Nobody should have to stoop to clean up after me or my family, anywhere.

So, why is it that being a handmaiden or a modern day Catherine Freemantle is still worth the cost of the loss of the pay cheque, and the independence and the status that comes with it?

The problem—and maybe the solution, but we will talk about that later—is that women do want it all. And in the world of paid work, as it is presently structured by men, that is not possible. Women want balance, men want success—read more money. Women want to move horizontally—they want time at home, time with their children and extended family, time for recreation, time for work, time for intellectual development, time for the successful career that was to flow from their education. Women want a balanced life that allows them to take their responsibilities seriously both at work and at home. Instead of feeling inadequate in both places they want to feel successful in both places.

Instead of moving horizontally, men want to move up. Upwards and onwards in their careers, earning more as they go. More grey hairs, more business lunch paunches, more heart attacks. Too many of these careers are a coronary in the making. The way in which men deploy themselves in terms of their jobs means taking time away from every other aspect of their lives. They might bemoan this fact but they rarely move to reshape their lives. They do not opt for part-time work, take jobs that have shorter commutes, or take equal responsibility for the day to day care of their children and extended family. That is their wife's work. Men are leading unbalanced lives and the stress and strain is killing them, even the ones who survive.

As Sayers understood, women with talents to offer to their communities, and responsibilities to exercise there, should not be confined to the home. But as we have seen the sharing of daily family maintenance within the home is still far from being equally divided between men and women to allow both equal access to the public sphere. This does indeed continue to constitute 'a damned waste!'

'Do you, personally, despise male criticism?'

'Heartily', said Miss Hillyard. 'But it does damage. Look at this University. All the men have been amazingly kind and sympathetic about the Women's Colleges. Certainly. But you won't find them appointing women to big University posts. That would never do. The women might perform their work in a way beyond criticism. But they are quite pleased to see us playing with our little toys.'

'Excellent fathers and family men,' murmured Harriet.

. . . 'Lor'!' said the Dean. 'That's Miss Hillyard's hobbyhorse. Rubbidge, as Mrs Gamp would say. Of course men don't like having their poor little noses put out of joint—who does? I think it's perfectly noble of them to let us come trampling over their University at all, bless their hearts. They've been used to being lords and masters for hundreds of years and they want a bit of time to get used to the change.'

Gaudy Night

Chapter 12
The Handmaiden: In the Office

Can you imagine a futuristic office building. Steel and chrome and marble and everywhere... glass. One of the most exciting architectural achievements of this building has been to take a time-tested feature, a staircase, and fashion it as a glass escalator; a feature for the use of male office workers only. When these men arrive at the top of the escalator their desks and their boardroom are placed upon a glass floor. Which actually doubles as a glass ceiling for the female workers below to gaze through. Fanciful? No, unfortunately, it is still fact.

It is still true, as Miss Hillyard adverts, that it is men who, having ridden the glass escalator, still hold the top positions in all our institutions, from universities to banks, from hospitals to courtrooms, from parliaments to factories. Men are still reluctant to appoint women to the top jobs. Women are still banging their heads off the glass ceiling, a metaphor coined by two journalists in the *Wall Street Journal* in 1986 to describe a reality observed by Sayers fifty years earlier.[1]

Twenty-five years later the figures on women and corporations remain deeply unsatisfactory. In the United States, among Fortune 500 companies, women occupy only fifteen percent of Board seats and are a mere three percent of CEOs. In Canada, the figures are almost the same; women occupy fourteen percent of Board seats and hold four percent of CEO jobs at Financial Post 500 businesses. There are only four female CEOs leading the 100 most highly capitalised blue chip companies listed on the London Stock Exchange, while only ten percent of Board seats in Europe at large are held by women. And even

---

1. C Hymowitz and TD Schellhardt, *The Glass Ceiling*, The Wall Street Journal. Special Report on Corporate Women, 24 March 1986.

this figure is skewed as a result of Norway's strict boardroom diversity laws where the number of women on boards jumped dramatically to forty-four percent in 2008.[2]

Facts like these from around the world are outlined in the report, 'Pipeline's Broken Promise', which surveyed more than 4,100 women and men from Europe, Asia, Canada and the USA. These employees worked full-time and had graduated from MBA programs between 1996 and 2007. The report found that women are paid on average US$4,600 less than men in their first post-MBA job and men start their first post-MBA job at higher positions than women. In the years that followed men's salary growth outpaced women's. Even when they both started at an entry level position, men rode that glass escalator more quickly up the corporate ladder. These inequities in both pay and rate of progress persist regardless of the global region in which they manifested, the number of years of prior experience or the industry in which they occurred. Furthermore, the parenthood status of these men and women made no difference, nor did the fact that the women expressly aspired to the same positions and level of advancement as the men. Not only is the corporate work place sexist, it is also racist. Women of colour fare even worse due to the persistence of race-based stereotypes.

Women had been told for so long that it was simply a pipeline problem: That more women would reach the top as more women entered the workforce. This 'trickle up' theory cannot be substantiated. Think how little has changed from Sayer's time to our own, at the very best a mere fifteen percent. Even then, a report compiled by consultants, Egon Zehnder International revealed what it described as systemic bias against female directors, saying they were often viewed as token or symbolic appointments.[3]

If the Glass Ceiling is so thick what are the issues that perpetuate it? The first is what is well known as the Old Boys Club. Even when men in the top jobs are not obviously sexist—and many of them have come to accept that this would land them into a lot of hot water—they still feel more comfortable with one of their own. Women are

---

2. Ilene H Lang, 'Have Women Shattered the Glass Ceiling?', in *USA Today*, 14 April 2010

3. Egon Zehnder International, "Women on European Boards", 3rd Biennial Monitor, 2008

not invited to grab a beer after work or a call-girl in Singapore. Not to mention the deals that are done on the golf courses of the world. Women are not invited into the networks where the boys make decisions about the boys and for the good of the boys.

Second, it is assumed that women will not stay the course, that they lack commitment. Three considerations show this argument to be unfounded. One is that it is lack of opportunity, not commitment, that will push women away. What is the point in working and working and never being rewarded? Another is that men get pregnant and have children too but they fail to take the same degree of responsibility for the daily care of their children. When was the last time you heard a senior male executive being asked, 'How long after the birth before you plan to go back to work?' The same holds true when it comes to the care of their elderly parents. They can't really, can they, because they are doing the top job. Finally, as we have learned from the Egon Zehnder study, even when women loudly vocalise their desire for the top job they do not get it. Frankly, I think men are just afraid to give women that much power and money. As Miss Hillyard said, "The women might perform their work in a way beyond criticism". They might even do it better than their male counterparts.

Third, there is the problem of the pay gap. This of course so often flows from the fact that the top man sees the aspiring woman as less committed because she is paid less, so you pay her less because she is less committed! The *Business Week*, April 2007, reported that American women earn eighty percent of what men earn in their first year out of college. The figure drops to sixty-nine percent when they are both ten years out of college. According to a more recent study from the White House Council for Economic Advisers, reported in the U.S News, October 31st, 2014, nothing has changed. If anything the figures are slightly worse with women now only earning 78% of men's earnings.

Finally, this leads us full circle to observe that there are not enough female role models. Either for women, who want to be like these successful women, or for the men in the top jobs so that they can see how effective, committed and valuable are women as CEOs and Board members. Mind you, it is hard to gain the necessary experience when you lack opportunity. If women are not given the opportunities to gain additional competencies they will find it hard to acquire the skills, such as specific managerial experience required to compete for, and be awarded, positions equal to those held by men and so close the pay gap. The Old Boys Club is rarely open for new membership.

Unless, of course, they need a woman to stand at the edge of the Glass Cliff. This is a senior job or important project given to a woman because it has a higher risk of failure. It would be unthinkable to blight the prospects of one of your Club mates by giving him the opportunity to become captain of a sinking ship. In a study conducted by the University of Exeter is was found that in FTSE 100 companies in the UK most women who were appointed to senior positions were handed this poisoned chalice only after a downturn in the company's fortunes which left them standing precariously at the edge of said Glass Cliff.[4]

There are still those, some of them women who have already achieved high ranking corporate positions, who would argue that the glass ceiling is no more. Jenny Seabrook, a Perth based company director who has served on the boards of some of Western Australia's biggest companies, is one such woman. She states, 'I'm not an advocate for a woman getting a position just because there's a target. I think it's very demeaning of women, and I think if you speak with most women they will agree'.[5] I think most women will agree that a woman should not get a position if she is not qualified for it. But a man does not feel demeaned if he gets a job in place of another man, both of whom are equally qualified, so why should a woman?

Because of what we have already discovered about how difficult it is for women to ride the glass escalator to the top, how much prejudice and how many unexamined assumptions are made about their lack of commitment, it seems essential that new strategies are adopted. In Australia a quarter of a century has passed since sex discrimination laws came into force. Since that time only 20.1% of directors of ASX200 Boards are women. The Australian Institute of Company Directors wants this figure to increase to thirty percent for all companies by 2018. However, the Director Resource Centre states

4. Drs Michele Ryan and Alex Haslem, University of Exeter, School of Psychology, 'The Glass Cliff: Evidence that Women Over-Represented in Precarious Leadership Positions', in the *British Journal of Management*, 16/2 (2005): 81–90

5. Williams, Ruth. 'New Focus Women on Boards: Gender Mender on Agenda', in *The Age,* 11 December 2009.

that appointments to the boards of ASX All Ordinaries at the end of July 2015 is a mere 15.4%. It is hard to see that figure doubling in two years.

Although men 'have been used to being lords and masters for hundreds of years', as Miss Hillyard reminds us, it seems that enough time might now have passed for men 'to get used to the change' and start sharing these corporations with their sisters. The first step would be for companies themselves to set targets over a period of three to five years. If this in unsuccessful then quotas should be imposed by governments to redress the existing inequitable balance. France, Spain, Germany and Norway have already taken this course. Norway's experiments with quotas boosted the proportion of women on Boards from seven percent to forty percent in five years changing forever the mental image of women's abilities in that country.

The good news is that adding women to the mix makes companies more profitable. A lot more profitable. A 2004 study by the world's largest association devoted to human resource management shows that those companies who have organised to break through the glass ceiling have prospered financially. In the United States, 353 out of Fortune 500 companies, those with the highest representation of women on their top management teams, had better financial performance than did the group with the lowest representation of women. The Return on Equity (ROE) was thirty-five percent higher and the Total Return to Shareholders (TRS) was thirty-four percent higher.[6] At the end of 2009, a Goldman Sachs report found that closing the gap between female and male employment across all sectors would boost Australia's gross domestic product by eleven percent. Why is the problem still so far from being solved?

Clearly, as these figures indicate, there are men who now understand that 'gender diversity' (they mean sexual equality) is the way forward. Perhaps where once there was only competition, women are adding a healthy dose of consensus. Given the sorry state of the world's financial markets and institutions since 2008 it seems like a good idea for more corporate men to engage in a little humility, admit that it was they who 'put their poor little noses out of joint', and turn to the ablest women in their companies to aid the recovery.

---

6.   Lockwood, Nancy. 'The Glass Ceiling: Domestic and International Perspectives', in *Society for Human Research Management, Research Quarterly*, 2004.

Here's our young lady clerk—I don't say she wasn't a good worker—but a whim comes over her and away she goes to get married, leaving me in the lurch, just when Mr. Urquhart is away. Now, with a young man, marriage steadies him, and makes him stick closer to his job, but with a young woman, it's the other way about. It's right she should get married, but it's inconvenient, and in a solicitor's office one can't get temporary assistance very well. Some of the work is confidential, of course, and, in any case, an atmosphere of permanence is desirable.'

Strong Poison

Chapter 13
The Pregnant Worker

About mid way in history between when Sayers was writing and today, I got a job as a waitress in a Dublin hotel. We had to provide our own uniforms, some form of brown skirt and white blouse. The cheapest garment I could find was a shapeless, brown smock. I was called into the manager's office and asked if I was pregnant. I told him I was not and he told me to go and buy something that did not make me look as if I were. The unspoken threat was, of course, that fecund meant fired. Where was the logic or the sense in this, I asked him. If pregnant women could come into the restaurant to eat why couldn't a pregnant woman serve them? Mind you, if I had been a young woman who needed this job to feed my family, I would not have dared ask him this question.

Very recently, a friend of my daughter, a solicitor and six months pregnant, was very relieved that she was not 'showing' because she had asked for a pay rise and feared she would not get it if her pregnancy became known. Lack of commitment and availability, she felt certain, was what she would be told. Her husband was a solicitor too but he was now in a very strong position to secure a pay rise on the grounds that he was starting a family. If female solicitors want to take their turn having babies why should male solicitors, who already have children, get angry with them? Why let these women get a degree and be admitted to practice? Maybe when they swear to uphold justice they should also swear not to marry a man who wants children.

Nobody gets angry with male solicitors when they have babies. For the simple reason that the vast majority of them take no time away from the office to care for their newborns. It would never have occurred to them, or, in fairness, to their wives. The pregnant worker only comes in one sex. As Joan Williams has described it, the problem for most women is that they never get near the glass ceiling because long before that they are stopped by 'the maternal wall'.[1]

The problem is that daily life is still not shared equally between husbands and wives. By this, I do not mean that they agree to work in paid employment for forty hours a week and both do twenty hours of housework. If they want to arrange life that way, no problem. If either of them wants to be a full-time, stay at home parent, no problem there either. The problem arises when maternity hits and paternity doesn't even notice.

That sounds harsh but let us look at a much quoted article written in 2003 by Lisa Belkin for *The New York Times*. The essay is entitled 'The Opt-Out Revolution', which, at one level, deals extremely well with exactly what the title suggests. It examines in detail the stories of several highly educated women who leave excellent jobs to go home to care for their children and their husbands. The fact that their husbands were equally well paid made the decision possible. But the context of these women's lives, beyond their families, is not examined. The backdrop, quite simply, is that the hours at the top are crazy and that their husbands, who also work these hours, rarely question this irrational system, certainly not to the extent of leaving their jobs.

Because this context is not analysed, the responses of Belkin's interviewees are sometimes superficial or even illogical. Each of the women hold the unexamined assumption that if 'they' have a baby, 'she' must take primary responsibility for its daily care. For example, one woman, Sally, a journalist married to a journalist, went back to work after her son was born. Some time later, she and her husband both crossed the country to cover the trial of OJ Simpson in California. 'I got mum and dad to bring Will (their son) out . . . I was determined not to blink.' Having a child was not going to stop Sally pursuing her career as she has always done. Yet, Sally had already blinked by thinking of herself as the parent responsible for making the child care arrangements. Likewise, it is hard to imagine her husband saying, or even thinking, that he 'was determined not to blink'.

Then there is the case of Katherine, extremely successful in her law career and an associate at a New York law firm. One day her

---

1. Joan C Williams and Nancy Segal, 'Beyond the Maternal Wall', in *Harvard Women's Law Journal*, 26 (2003).

husband is offered a job in Atlanta. We are told that this change was particularly appealing to Katherine because it offered her something Manhattan could not—an easy commute: 'I could practice law in a top firm and still be only ten minutes from home. It seemed like an ideal way to have children and a career.' There are several questions not touched upon in this account. Would her husband have left his job in New York and moved to Atlanta for her? Was an 'easy commute' that would bring him home in ten minutes a determining factor in job choice for him? Was he consciously looking for an ideal way to combine children and a career? Much more likely, he simply assumed that he would pursue his career uninterrupted and somehow she would find a way to take care of any children.

The crazy hours and the pressure eventually got to both Sally and Katherine. They both wanted to continue working so they asked for shorter hours. There is no record of their husbands looking for part-time work. Katherine wanted to become a partner but when she admitted to her husband that if she achieved this ambition then 'financially it gets better, but in terms of my actual life, it gets worse'. Again, there is no record of him asking, 'What can I do to help you become a partner? How can I make sure your life doesn't get worse?' There is no hint that he said to her, 'It's not fair that your life should get worse and mine continue as before'. Predictably, Sally and Katherine quit. In their repeated attempts to balance both areas of their lives they felt under pressure and unable to do either job well.

Another story is that of Vicky. She speaks for many when she says, 'I never felt discriminated against in any way'. However, after marriage, she took a step down by joining a less high-profile firm. She made this choice, she says, 'because I knew the long-term career was going to be his'. Does this knowledge really equate with never feeling discriminated against in any way? There are deep-seated and unexamined assumptions at work here, assumptions about a man's and a woman's proper place in the world.

But then Vicky says something very interesting: 'I like life's rhythms when I'm nurturing a child'. Which is exactly what Katherine and Sally wanted. To be the kind of parent they wanted to be *and* to have a career. They wanted it all; to rearrange the workplace so that they could employ their talents and training and care for their children. It appears to be the most rational and caring plan you could draw up.

This desire does not seem to be asking a lot: for a woman to be the kind of parent she wants to be and have a career. There is not a father alive who would not say the same thing. The problem is that he is happy to leave the child-raising to someone else, his wife or the nanny or the granny. He will be available as often as work permits. Which is the companion problem—work rarely permits, for either of them.

I think Belkin is correct when she says, 'As these women look up at the 'top', they are increasingly deciding that they don't want to do what it takes to get there'. Why don't the husbands decide this too? Why would you want to work twelve to fifteen hours a day, six days a week? You are too tired to be good company for your partner, your small children are asleep before you get home, making time for your siblings or your parents is almost a chore and your friends are neglected. Women can see very clearly that life without love, fun and relaxation is a life not worth living but their men do not share this vision. It is only the women who are not willing to take time away from everything precious in life to earn a cold fortune.

Many of the women who 'opt-out' are coming up with a new equation. Success is no longer determined or gauged by money but by balance. Somebody once said there is a time for everything under Heaven and these women do, finally, understand what could be meant by having everything.

As they studied, and strove, and pushed, and placated, they launched themselves into the world of men. They were successfully assimilated if not entirely successful. They started out their working lives fretting that life was getting in the way of work. In the end, they realised that work was getting in the way of life.

Too many of the husbands are failing to 'opt-out'. They are still beguiled by the system they have created, by the prospect of more money, which, in turn, brings more power. The more they have of these two commodities the more successful they believe themselves to be. So does most of the rest of the world. Money and power are not bad in and of themselves but the way they are being exercised in the pursuit of global capitalism is killing the players, not to mention the planet.

Men and women behave differently alright. But it is not prescribed they were not born that way. If women can do all the things that men do—and we have seen clearly in the stories of Sally and Katherine and Vicky that they can—then men can do all the things that women can do. To date, we are familiar with the female/mother/caregiver but the male/father/caregiver is equally possible. Men are equally able to care and nurture and achieve balance in their lives. If they choose. There is no glass ceiling in the nursery or the kitchen. He says, no thanks, that's not where I want to operate. Well, think about it, Sally and Katherine and Vicky do not want to operate there all the time either. They too want fulfilling jobs that are paid, bringing them financial independence, especially if their husbands run off with a younger model.

A note of caution needs to be inserted here. Nearly any professional woman that you talk to will say, 'I'm opting-out temporarily. I want to be with my children when they are small. My maternity leave might go on for five years but I have every intention of going back, either full or part-time.' That is a good plan, if you can make it work. But the work place goes roaring on, getting busier and faster and because the glass ceiling is still well and truly in place, there are no women at the top to change the shape of the system, to make it more humane, to mandate a work/life balance.

Of course, there will always be those men who give everything to their careers, and who have permission to be this way because of our long history of gender stereotyping. There will be women too, almost always without children, who follow the path to the top. Nonetheless, there are cracks appearing. As we have seen, many companies are insisting on gender diversity because of the increase in their profitability. As women take top jobs and then leave, men are learning that it can be done without their beards ceasing to grow.

All of our female friends might have been happier if they and their husbands could have shared the children's early years while all of them maintained their careers. All these professional men and women might be a great deal happier if, instead of women being assimilated into a distorted system, they could point the way to liberation. Women's liberation could then give birth to men's liberation! At last. To paraphrase Sayers, maybe what is most desirable of all, what most smacks of liberation is the desire for an atmosphere of permanent balance.

. . . through that hot unhappy year when she had tried to believe there was happiness in surrender.

Gaudy Night

Chapter 14
Sexual Harassment

It is not uncommon to find that authors have written their truth into their fiction. So it is with Dorothy Sayers. In her novel, *Strong Poison*, she tells us that Harriet Vane fell in love with Philip Boyes and agreed to live with him because Philip did not believe in marriage. Sayers too agreed to live with her lover who also did not believe in marriage although she wanted to marry and have children. While the revealing words are placed in the mouth of Harriet, they come straight out of Sayer's own life: 'Through that hot unhappy year when she tried to believe that there was happiness in surrender', Sayers became pregnant and gave birth to a son. Her lover abandoned her.

If there is one theme that runs through stories of rape and sexual harassment it is that women nearly always feel worse when they have sought justice by reporting the incident. Time after time, you hear that breaking the silence produces an outcome that is worse for the woman than silence. This is because both rape and harassment are more about power than about sex. That is obvious because men harass down, selecting women who are in positions of less power than themselves. The domination becomes most obvious when the harasser sets out to punish the victim for complaining. She gets poor grades or fails to pass exams, she is not promoted or maybe even fired.

Exactly what constitutes sexual harassment has been hard to define. Particularly because the complaint is so often belittled. 'Can't you take a joke; he was only stealing a kiss'. It is generally defined as a type of employment discrimination consisting of verbal or physical abuse of a sexual nature, although it can also take place in educational situations. What behaviour translates into harassment and the nature of the relationship between the parties is always a question of fact in each case. However, within the justice system, harassment has generally been divided into two types. The first is *Quid Pro Quo* harassment where someone in a position of power, almost always a man, demands sexual favours in return for advancement. This form of harassment is not difficult to prove but it is uncommon compared to the other form, 'hostile environment' harassment. In these cases, and again it is mostly women who are the victims, the environment becomes toxic for them due to unwelcome sexual jokes, seeing pornographic pictures, repeated requests for dates, being inappropriately touched or brushed against. There is no threat to promotion here or danger of being fired, at least not overtly, but the women are subjected to a degree of psychological strain that alters the terms and conditions of their jobs.

Whatever form it takes, it is hard to bring it out into the open. The reprisals range from the infantile, 'Oh, come on, where is your sense of humour?!' to the dangerous closing of ranks at the level of managers or deans or colonels. One such example was the outing by Naomi Wolf of Professor Harold Bloom at Yale University, when, 'famous, productive, revered' he was still teaching in the English department. She charged him with the sexual assault she had suffered twenty years previously. At the time she was twenty years of age, he was her teacher and he placed his hand on her inner thigh. And she never told because she knew that in making an accusation it was her word against his so what was the point in pursuing it. Like a rape victim, she had probably asked for it, and anyway, was it serious enough? Would it affect the teacher/student relationship in terms of her grades? What about his reputation and career?

The story ends in 2004 when Wolf wrote an article for the *New York Magazine*. Wolf believed that she had an obligation to other victims and that she had failed them because, as she says of herself, she had 'not been brave enough' when she was at school, partly because she was impecunious. She did not want to sue Bloom, or Yale. All she wanted was to be sure that the Grievance Board was effective and the institution was accountable. The response that this Yale graduate and Rhodes scholar received was silence, obfuscation and denial. As a last resort she went public.

Wolf came to understand, she writes, that if the institution knows of a faculty member's tendency to make sexual approaches to students, and it fails to take corrective action, then it may be responsible for condoning a hostile environment. Bloom's action was not demonic; Wolf was not a victim. But corporations and universities and armed forces need to legislate what to do about people, nearly always men, who behave improperly. When they are guilty of an abuse of power they need to pay. As Wolf wryly observes, 'Powerful men and women who belittle and humiliate their subordinates manage not to belittle and humiliate their superiors'.

At the end of her article, Wolf admits that if a young female student came to her with a similar complaint, she could not recommend, even by 2004, that she go to the Grievance Board to secure a just hearing: 'Wishing that [then-President of Yale] Bart Giamatti's beautiful welcoming speech to my class about Yale's meritocracy were really true, I would, with a heavy heart, advise that young woman, for her own protection, to get a good lawyer'.

Even then the law may not be the place to find justice. Those who bring complaints of sexual harassment have to prove that they have been harmed emotionally. Their lawyers will try and ferret out nightmares, post traumatic stress, sexual dysfunction, any trauma at all so that the focus is on the legally necessary frailty of the complainant. Feeling furiously angry and not a bit frail is not the answer when dealing with the law of Torts. What you must prove is that you have suffered all sorts of emotional harm. Instead, the focus should be upon the frailty, inadequacy and ineffectiveness of the institution in failing to take care of the student, the worker or the soldier. It should not only be a question of how much in the way of damages is to be paid to the complainant but a question of what are we going to do to restore the reputation and social standing of the company, the university or the armed services.

If we move to turn the spotlight onto the accountability of the institution then we can stop asking questions like, what were you wearing? That question is still out there but what is wrong with women dressing to attract men?

A current setting within which to address this question is the blossoming of marches known as, intending to shock, Slut Walks. All around the globe, from Toronto to Washington, from Glasgow to Sydney and on to Delhi women are organising again. The point of this movement is to put an end to blaming victims either for their behaviour or clothing or both for the sexual violence and harassment that is meted out to them.

The intent of the Slut Walks, to stop blaming the victim, and its provocative name, arose in Toronto directly from the comment of a police officer who told a group of students at Osgoode Hall Law School that if they wanted to avoid rape then they should 'avoid dressing like sluts'. Constable Michael Sanguinetti was trying to be helpful and had no idea, or wish, that his victim blaming gaffe would make him this famous.

How do you reclaim the word, 'slut'? It is certainly a powerful one; undeniably, it makes you sit up and take notice. Some have suggested it is too shocking yet words can be reclaimed. The homosexual community adopted the words 'gay' and 'queer' and have successfully deprived them of their negative power. Nearly a century ago, we had Emmeline Pankhurst chaining herself to the rails in London and, more recently, Germaine Greer burning bras in Sydney. Most men and women had little good to say of either of them at the time. Yet, however shocking or unpopular, someone always has to break new ground and plow a furrow that makes it easier for the rest of us to follow. The pendulum will spring back but in the meantime, however extreme you think the clothes and the language, the movement has created a global dialogue in which women feel free to discuss sexual assault and harassment without fear of blame.

At this point in the history of dictionaries, the word 'slut' is still defined as a slovenly or promiscuous woman. But the young, feminist women on these marches are anything but that. Some of them do want to wear mini skirts, fishnet stockings and paint the word 'slut' on their t-shirts, but that, along with the name of the movement, is primarily to attract attention to the cause. This is a perfectly valid approach to consciousness raising. The contrary point of view, held by older women, who no longer wear short skirts, is that the task of this movement should be to critique and reform the societal structures that support sexual violence. They argue that this cause is not helped by frivolous names and clothing where the political goal could get lost in the personal claim of the right to wear whatever I want to.

Both positions are valid, but the young women are not wrong because the question of what a woman wears continues to be central to discussions of sexual violence. In 1999 Italy's highest court ruled that a woman wearing jeans could not be raped because it was impossible to remove a pair of jeans 'without the collaboration of the person wearing them'. In February 2011 a Manitoba judge, Robert Dewar, condemned a rape survivor in court for wearing a tube top, no bra, high heels and makeup. He implied that her clothing led to the assault because the rapist, 'a clumsy Don Juan', succumbed to 'inviting circumstances'.

It is unfortunate and embarrassing that sometimes women can be even more misinformed and judgmental than men. One such is the English columnist, Melanie Phillips. She believes that these SlutWalks prove that feminism is now irrelevant to most women's lives.[1] Arguing from the same faulty premises as the Italian and Canadian judges, Phillips asserts that the SlutWalkers have dressed themselves as 'sex objects . . . in the most sexually provocative manner possible'. It seems that the walker is 'sending a signal that she wants to be leered at or phantasised about'. But Phillips is not correct: there is no such thing as 'provocative dressing' or 'revealing clothing'. There is no standard fixed in time by which to decipher these phrases.

Times change attitudes. Was it shocking and immodest when women first wore evening gowns cut away at the back, down to their waists, in Sayers' time? Goodness, not long before that she was not permitted to display her ankle. The neck to knee bathing suit of one age, once thought so appropriately modest, would now be considered bizarre by the bikini and budgie smuggler brigade on Bondi Beach. In fact, the women of Sydney are rather overdressed compared to those wearing only a thong on the beach at Ipanema. Phantasising and chastising are in the mind and eye of the beholder. My Muslim taxi driver in Damascus told me that women—robed from head to toe—could not worship with the men because the men might get sexually excited if a woman was to kneel in submission with her forehead on the ground in front of him. If clothing is the problem, then why are small children and old women, all appropriately dressed, being raped?

Nowhere do the SlutWalkers insist that clothing has no effect on people. Young men and women spend hours, and small fortunes, deciding which clothes make them look most attractive, and have the greatest possible effect, on the opposite sex. They do not dress to be

---

1. Phillips, Melanie. 'These SlutWalks Prove Feminism is Now Irrelevant to Most Momen's Lives', *The Daily Mail*, 13 June 2011.

leered at. They dress to impress. None of this is about 'prudence', it is all about fashions.

Phillips does not have a clear grasp of even the basics of feminist theory. Nowhere do the SlutWalkers insist that 'women's behaviour never contributes to any harm that may befall them'. Feminists, like most right thinking people, take personal responsibility as a given. As feminists they are dressing to attract men, not to be raped or harassed by them. They are asking men, to use Phillips' own words, to take 'responsibility for their own actions which lies at the heart of being a human being'. To be a political activist and to wear the word 'slut' on your t-shirt as part of an organised political demonstration is to say, I have a right to wear what I like and be safe from rape and sexual harassment.

Phillips concludes with the assertion that 'modern feminism has been a powerful factor in that dismal process' which has degraded the whole notion of human sexuality. This is Phillips getting things upside down. It was men who argued for centuries that women were less than human, inadequate in reason and whose sole purpose was reproduction. Where man was mind, woman was body and she should make herself available for 'predatory means of self-gratification' for the benefit of men. Modern feminism has been a powerful factor in the struggle to rid men of these ill-conceived notions and to redress the balance to provide a mutual and loving respect between the sexes. The sooner men can grasp, what should really be considered self-evident, that women are never 'asking for it', for rape or harassment, the sooner we will reach that goal.

Feminism, too infrequently adverted to, is a body of knowledge that is of the utmost relevance to the productive and moral lives of *all* women *and* men.

If the woman took the view that any husband was better than none at all, it was useless to argue.

Gaudy Night

Chapter 15
The Single Woman: Married or Not

In the world in which I grew up the single life was never presented as an option. You got married or became a nun. Choosing to stay single was apparently a life without purpose.

I meet many women, every year, who think that 'any husband is better than none at all'. I know this because they hold two completely unexamined assumptions, the one following from the other. The first is that they will get married, they must, their whole future happiness depends upon it. The second is that if something goes horribly wrong and they do not marry, then they will be a sad and lonely creature, an object of sympathy to the world at large, unwanted, a failure. Without a man they are nothing, not in their own eyes, or, they believe, in the eyes of the world.

By the time I meet these women they have arrived at a point of great anxiety. They are afraid of being alone, they hate being an object of sympathy and their biological clock is ticking, ticking. They come with the question: How can I meet a man? The question is never posed quite that baldly but a husband is unquestionably the topic of interest. I answer them with another question: Perhaps you are asking me, how can I be happy in life?

What follows now is a very different take on how to be a woman in the world. It begins a conversation that suggests starting the search for happiness not by finding a man but by finding yourself. Not looking without but seeking within.

Many single women assume that they are not enough; that somehow, in and of themselves, they are incomplete, inadequate, uninteresting. Without thinking about it they are convinced they could never be happy alone. They know that there is a big empty space inside of them that can only be filled by someone else. Which leads to a feeling of quiet desperation, with the need to love and be loved, to possess and be possessed. Like the merging of two candle flames at a wedding ceremony there is the confused notion that being fused with another is the way to find themselves. Fusion means certainty and safety. Just like Heathcliff in *Wuthering Heights* they want to break down the barrier between the self and the other. Heathcliff was obsessed with Cathy and with the desire to make her his own, even to the point of willing that one side of their coffins be cut off so that they cold lie together through all eternity. Out of contact with reality, he could not see that Cathy might ever have different wishes and needs of her own. In the person of Heathcliffe, Emily Brontë draws one of the best examples in western literature of the person who has never learned to love themselves, of the person who looks without rather than within to find themselves.

Learning to love ourselves is the first step to a happy and healthy life. This is not new news, it is a message that has been repeated over and over again until it seems to us so trite that it cannot be true. Yet it is the truest, most profound and most important lesson we will ever learn. Learning to love ourselves is not easy. It is, in fact, very difficult, particularly if you are a female. Even if a girl has been raised throughout her childhood and adolescence being told by her parents what a wonderful person she is, how loveable she is, how important and valuable she is, this message is constantly contradicted by the wider world. It is so difficult, this learning to love ourselves, that we frequently fail and run about in ever decreasing circles, searching frantically for someone else to love. This is never the place to begin because a step in that direction is, in reality, the quest for someone who will love and admire us, make us feel valuable, fill up that empty space, and give us what we think we lack. When you think about it for a minute, you will see how illogical that is: We want someone to give us what we cannot give to ourselves because we know we are not worthy of the gift.

So, it stands to reason, literally, that self love must come first. When we love ourselves, we are gentle with ourselves, not judgmental. At the same time we are willing to take responsibility for ourselves, to be self-critical in a positive and reflective sense. We are accepting of our weaknesses and forgiving of our failures. We can delight in our talents, valuing each one of them. We take care of our bodies. Self-knowledge will go hand in hand with self-respect. Self love is essential if we live our lives alone and it is essential if we live in an intimate relationship because only in this condition are we fit to share ourselves, as a whole person, with someone else.

It was the other Brontë, Emily's sister, Charlotte, who gave us such an enduring and endearing example of self love in her heroine, Jane Eyre. Jane finds work as a governess in Rochester's household. He wants to make her his mistress so Jane, respecting herself, leaves him. She is befriended by two sisters, whose brother is a parson about to leave England for the West Indian missions. He wants Jane to go with him, not because he truly loves her but because she is a good person and will be his good helpmate. Jane loves herself well enough to know her true value and so, as she left the 'bad' man who did not love her, Jane now leaves the 'good' one. Even though, note well, she is destitute. Then hearing Rochester crying out to her, she hurries back to find his house on fire and he blinded by a falling beam. In his blindness, Rochester can see Jane for who she really is and Jane can help Rochester learn to love himself.

It is only when we come home to ourselves, regain our ego-boundaries that we can then begin falling in love in the real sense. Heathcliff had lost his, despising himself. Jane was fully aware of hers, valuing herself and requiring that she be respected for who she was. One story ends in tragedy while Jane and Rochester can live happily ever after. As Margaret Anderson puts it so succinctly: 'In real love you want the other person's good. In romantic love you want the other person.'

Mind you, it is often this 'happily ever after' that gets us into so much trouble. We are so sure that if we can just find the right person we really will live in married bliss forever. It is with this idealism about love and marriage that our chapter began. Yet, the last time I looked there were twenty-seven varieties of family in the Republic of Ireland. Not bad for a tiny, predominately Catholic population. The mum and dad, 'married but once and then to each other', who both live with all their children is no longer the norm as the configuration of what it means to be a family is constantly changing. Married or cohabiting, straight or gay, divorced and remarried, childless, adoptive, fostering, the permutations are multiple.

Talking about families often leads to talking about contraception. In the late 60s, the early years of the feminist movement, an idea that was indeed revolutionary was propounded: women had sexual needs just like men, and what's more they enjoyed having them met. It was obvious that if women wanted to share the sexual freedoms that men had always enjoyed they needed effective contraception. The social conservatives saw the pill as the beginning of a sexual revolution and they were not wrong. If women were able to separate sex from procreation then the fear of pregnancy no longer inhibited women's sexual lives. With the fear of pregnancy removed, single women could have sex at will and married women could have affairs. The control of fertility meant that women could now have sex anywhere, anytime with anyone just as men had always done.

Imagine the single woman, imbued with a healthy dose of self love and with the means to control her fertility in her handbag. She is educated and has as much chance as a man to be employed (if not always paid as much or promoted to the same level) and own her own home. Is she happy? Again, no more or less than her male counterpart. The challenge is for both of them to find out what their lives are about. Who are they, what do they most enjoy doing, where can they make a difference, what is the purpose of being alive at all for them. You might even say that in answering these questions they are in the process of discerning a vocation.

Once they are all settled, both men and women, at least for the time being, on their chosen path then, and only then, might they start to think about finding someone with whom to share a life that is *already* full and committed. It is amazing just how attractive the energised, purposeful, happy person appears.

On the other hand, some women might decide that what they want in life is not a partner but a child to whom they can gift the blessings they have received. Despite the availability of contraception the incidence of lone parenthood has risen steadily. In Australia the 2009–2010 census figures revealed that nineteen percent of all families were single parent families, and of these eighty-five percent were headed by mothers.[1] According to the census data for Ireland by 2006 the number of lone parent families with children under the age

---

1. Australian Bureau of Statistics, 444.2 Family Characteristics, Australia, 2009–2010. www.abs.gov.au

of fifteen accounted for 21.3% of the families. However, before blindly advocating single parenthood it is necessary to be aware that analysis of these figures also reveals that these families are at the same risk of poverty as were the two parent families with over four children that were so common in previous decades.

But if women can afford to raise a child then there is no reason why they should not choose to do so. Especially when we know how many fathers walk away from their children and their financial responsibility for them. These deserted women, wives or girlfriends or even one night stands, are left, literally, holding the baby. They must raise these children unless they decide to adopt or abort. After all, nobody would suggest that a widow was unable to raise her child alone. Or describe her as an unmarried, single mother in a broken family. Widowers take note; you too can be a single parent.

I would suggest that because the social revolution has already taken place, certainly in the developed world, what we need is public policy that supports the legitimacy of the diverse family structures that already exist all about us. There is no call to privilege the two-parent, heterosexual, married family when we know that children are born or adopted into very happy, unmarried, homosexual relationships, either gay or lesbian.

The legal unit of the married mother and father is no more natural than any other family form. Simply asserting it does not make it so. Certainly, there are those who would argue that a father is necessary to provide a role model for his children. The proponents of this position are especially keen to insist that little boys need a father to provide a masculine role model. There is no reason to see mothering and fathering as distinct social roles that cannot be interchanged. It is perfectly natural to be raised by one parent if the other one dies or deserts. Or to be raised by your grandparents if both parents die. Or to be adopted by a lesbian if you are left in an orphanage.

This is not to say that if you were raised by your father alone or mother alone the experience would be a different one. This difference, however, is not judgmental. It does not mean that one parent does it better than the other simply by virtue of their sex. Fathers do have a unique role to play, as do mothers, but being unique is not the same as being essential. Both sexes are equally able to care for and raise healthy, well balanced offspring. To say otherwise is to agree with the conventional wisdom that denigrates fathers.

Furthermore, should these biological parents marry, there is no reason to believe that the childcare would automatically be of a higher standard. Marriage can be a very dubious social institution and is no better or worse than the couple who form it. It can be the site of as much brutality and deprivation as it can be a haven of love and nurturance. Marriages that are genuinely destructive of either or both parents and of children are better ended, for everyone involved.

Each of us has a responsibility to develop our own talents, to become the best possible person we can be. Our task, should we choose to accept it, is to find out what we were born to do and do it. It is never a 'mission impossible' but it is definitely a mission. The fact of being a human being requires of us that we come to fulness within each and every one of our relationships before we, perhaps, choose to enter one special relationship.

Is any husband better than none at all? Of course not. It is for this reason that I advocate the single life—married or not.

After all, what could he do? He was in exactly the same boat as herself. With a foolish relic of Victorianism she had somehow imagined that a man would display superior energy and resourcefulness, but, after all, he was only a human being, with the usual outfit of arms and legs.

Have His Carcase

Chapter 16
Woman as Entrepreneur: Power and Voice

One of the hardest things to do in life is to identify our own talents. Then begins the hard work of using them to claim *your* power and *your* voice.

I used to teach a course in ecofeminist philosophy and the word 'philosophy' made students very wary; they anxiously confided that they did not know any philosophy. I knew they were wrong. So we settled down to talk about how they viewed life and love and marriage and kids and schools and politics and the economy and prisons and the army and foreign policy and natural resources and global warming, they discovered that they knew a great deal about philosophy. And, appropriately, they had many more questions than they did answers.

True enough, they did not spend their lives systematically reflecting on these questions. They had not given birth to grand schemes of thought as did HobbEs or Hume or Hegel but daily life demanded that they come up with daily answers, however temporary, to their questions. They came to see that asking the right question was the most valuable contribution they could make to civic life. They were not professional philosophers but they were capable philosophers.

When it comes to entrepreneurs there is also a scale. At one end there are big and successful international ones like Dame Anita Roddick who started The Body Shop. Launching in 1976, quickly generating extraordinarily large turnover, boasting huge profits, and employing thousands of people, this international company has 2,400 stores—at last count—in sixty-one countries, making it the second largest cosmetic franchise in the world and now part of the *L'Oréal* corporate group. At the other end there are small and modest enterprises like that of Deborah, Duchess of Devonshire, selling the produce from the farm which she started around the time Sayers was writing. There are some, even smaller, begun with family money by persons still unknown, whose home-based industries, support their families.

We have been conditioned to thinking that 'big' and 'business' go together because it is an open secret that the big businesses are the ones that secretly control governments. They are also the ones most often in the news. We also know more business*men* than we do business*women*. Being a business man is an occupation; business women are an aberration. Suits were never called 'power suits' until women wore them to work. Yet women have been going into business by themselves as far back as we can remember. Women were dressmakers and milliners, hairdressers and caterers, and more recently, doctors and lawyers. In the same way that everyone is a philosopher, everyone has a money-making skill.

Businesses founded by women are not a new phenomenon but they are perhaps, as we will see, more important now than they have ever been. Recession is a time for survival rather than making millions. Everywhere in the developed world entrepreneurs are feeling the pinch of the economic downturn. Customers are saving their money rather than spending it and the banks are holding on to these savings rather than lending it to small businesses. This is particularly disappointing as this is precisely the moment when increased rates of corporate windups, with the ensuing unemployment, mean that there are more highly skilled and experienced staff available to create new enterprises.

Even so, the number of women who run businesses is growing. As these numbers grow more power is exerted by women and they are in a position to give more voice to their sisters in public life. When women get more voice in public life they get more voice in private life. When you are achieving as successfully as a man in the market place your man at home has to listen. You invert the old adage and the political becomes personal. In this happy circle of power relations, women can gain power and voice in every sphere of their lives.

One of the first investigations into this growing variant on what was once almost entirely an all male word was made in 1976 in the United States. Eleanor Schwartz's article, 'Entrepreneurship: A New

Female Frontier', was published in the *Journal of Contemporary Business*. At that time there were 700,000 women-owned businesses in the United States generating $41.5 million in revenues (United States Bureau of Census, 1977). By the turn of the century there were over nine million businesses owned by women. By 2003 women were a driving force in the United States economy.

In the United Kingdom there are approximately 620,000 majority women owned businesses with a turnover of £130 billion. In 2005, the then Chancellor of the Exchequer, Gordon Brown, noted that if the United Kingdom could achieve the same levels of female Entrepreneurship as the United States, Britain would gain three quarters of a million more businesses.

What was happening on both sides of the Atlantic was happening all around the globe. By 2010 the Global Entrepreneur Monitor was conducting research in fifty-nine economies worldwide.[1] For example, in that year the GEM report for Ireland confirmed that it is highly entrepreneurial and the rate of early stage activity in the country continues to be one of the highest in Europe: 8.6% of the adult population are established entrepreneurs which compares favourably with Australia (8.5%) and the United States (7.7%). However, men are nearly two and a half times more likely to be an early stage entrepreneur which approximates the norm for the European Union and OECD though substantially behind Australia and the United States.[2]

Despite the fact that there are still fewer women than men starting their own businesses there are several reasons why the number of entrepreneurial women is growing. Some of them, the fortunate, who are already financially independent are looking to put some purpose into their lives. As Sayers reminds us, Lord Peter Wimsey remarks to his sister, ' . . . you seem very much taken up with this house-decorating job you're running.' To which Lady Mary replies, 'One must do something. I get rather sick of being aimless, you know.'

Other women of means seek not only purpose but also independence. This seems evident when we see that the rate of female employment-to-self-employment migration far outstrips the rate

---

1. See www.gemconsortium.org
2. Paula Fitzsimons and Colm O'Gorman, 'The Annual Report for Ireland, Entrepreneurship in Ireland', *Global Entrepreneurship Monitor*, 2010.

at which women are moving into senior management roles. Many disappointed and frustrated women are seeking alternate ways of working. The reason is not hard to find. Entrepreneurship is clearly the way around the problem of the glass ceiling. Women who are talented and highly qualified are leaving corporate careers in their droves, many to set up their own businesses or work as consultants in their old field. If your hard work is not being appreciated, if you are being passed over for promotion again and again, eventually you will seek the freedom to succeed on your own.

The most commonly cited reasons for women's exit from corporate life are the desire for greater freedom, autonomy, work-life balance and professional development.[3]

The first gift of this new found autonomy is that you do not have to cast about, beyond yourself, reading the situations vacant ads, to find whatever jobs are on offer. No more do you have to twist yourself into any shape to fit the job. Once you have taken responsibility to identify your own talents you are then free to follow your bliss and shape a job that expresses them. When you look inside, you find what it is that you like to do and what you like to do you are usually very good at doing. I had a friend called Kevin Preston, who used to be a baker in Coolangatta. Tired, literally, of getting up at 4am, he started his own business which was, not surprisingly, a pie shop. The sign over his shop read, 'eat here or we'll both starve' but there was no danger; he made wonderful pies.

Avoiding starvation would not be setting the bar very high. It is true that achieving minimum goals would provide maximum flexibility but the personality of most entrepreneurs will have them working a little harder than that. At the same time there is no rule that you have to double your income every year for the rest of your life. When a woman works for herself she makes the rules of her own game. There is no manager demanding that you come in early and stay late, be the last car in the car park, work weekends and if you demur find your desk cleared on Monday morning. The corollary of course is that you and your employees can have more flexibility about the hours that you do work. This in turn leads straight to a more sane

---

3. N Patterson, and S Mavin, 'Women Entrepreneurs: Jumping the Corporate Ship and Gaining New Wings', in *International Small Business Journal*, 27/2 (2009): 173–192.

approach to work/life balance. You can work four days a week and spend Fridays with your parents. You can start early and be at the school gate at 3pm. You can take holidays. Beyond relentless toil there is room for imagination.

The contours of such a life, however you decide to shape it, has to be appealing. Unlike the person who is so determined to be in control that they lose control entirely, ceding their lives to gender stereotypes of culture, here lies independence.

Schwartz noted many similarities in the goals of male and female entrepreneurs. Women, like men, felt a 'need to achieve', to experience job satisfaction and independence. But where they differed was clearly gender specific. It was around 'growth patterns' and the setting of financial goals. These findings are not surprising. We saw in a previous chapter the cultural pressure on a woman to get a man and then to be the primary parent. Likewise, the pressure remains on a man to be in control and be successful. The best way to do both of those things is to make a lot of money, or at least, to be the primary breadwinner. At this point a man may have lost what he initially professed to want—freedom and autonomy. The last case may prove to be worst than the first. Fear of failure, or of turning away a customer who may not be replaced, may drive him to work harder than he did when he was the company man.

Finally, to understand professional development as an entrepreneurial goal is to recognise that we need help from others to reach our full potential. The most effective way that power and voice were transferred to the powerless and voiceless in the past was through the trade union. Trade unions face real difficulties in these times but they still make a difference to many. In the United States today, it is estimated that a Latina's wages increase by fifty percent for the same work when she joins a union; all women experience an increase of thirty-three percent for the same work when they join a union.

For women working in businesses or corporations that were not unionised, the way to professional development was paved by the advice of a mentor who helped with the social, emotional and personal growth needed to succeed in the job, whatever it was. While mentoring is still popular, it is also being upgraded by an idea whose time has definitely come: sponsorship. The Harvard Business

Review has defined sponsorship as the 'active support by someone appropriately placed in the organisation who has sufficient influence on decision-making processes or structures and who is advocating for, protecting and fighting for the career advancement of an individual'. This sounds very like the glass escalator that men have always ridden and it is clearly the way into the critical networks of your group. Of course, the further you rise the fewer the positions so sponsorship becomes even more essential to secure advancement at the highest levels.

We had thought that by now fathers would be parenting partners. Although they have not yet arrived at this point of equality in anything like sufficient numbers men must move in that direction. As we continue in the current downward economic spiral we need new hybrid models of work and family. Unemployment is high but the children still need to be taken care of so the answer seems obvious. As we balance the sharing of labour, in and outside the home, with the need to pursue independent interests, the role of primary breadwinner might move back and forth from one to the other, foregrounding certain talents at one point and others at another. Women are still teachers, nurses and social workers but they have also become CEO's, soldiers and secretaries of state. Men are going to have to expand their job horizons by taking on traditionally female occupations while also getting more involved at home. If men embraced parental leave women would be spared the 'mommy track' and the reduction in both pay cheque and pension that goes with it. When fathers are more involved with their children these children stay in school longer, steering clear of crime and avoiding poverty as adults.

What we have discovered, thanks to a recent study by the World Economic Forum, is that when we have an equal number of men and women in the work force the gross domestic product greatly increases. In the United States it was found to increase by as much as nine percent. Whatever happens, the workplace cannot remain so enduringly hostile to the needs of family life.

All these ideas can be, and have been, borrowed by entrepreneurial women in establishing, running and growing their businesses. This type of solidarity and networking are the hallmarks of the new ways in which women do business. They are obviously acutely aware that more responsibility for the family means less productivity and profit for women's firms. Women running their own businesses will tackle head on that burdensome lie that any one person can do it all. If you want to work and have children you cannot do it without being able to depend on a close network of helpers.

One way for women to run businesses differently is to fight classism as well as sexism. Because your office needs to be cleaned and because your employees need child care then managers should advertise these vacancies on the business web site beside the vacancy for an IT manager. If an employee brings in her sick neighbour's children to be minded in the office creche along with her own then make the necessary additional payment to the child minder. Feminists have always argued that cleaning and child minding is work so these workers should be treated as would all other employees on whom the business depends: they deserve holiday pay, sick days, personal days and severance notice and pay.

Entrepreneurship is the way out and up for many women. Feminism does not always have to be about issues or identity politics. We can shift the focus to changing the environment, to seek out ways in which we can do things differently, to make a space in which we can come up with new and innovative methods to make money and have a good time doing it. For women, and men, who are looking to balance work and family life and both sexes having 'the usual outfit of arms and legs', becoming an entrepreneur is one way forward.

Harriet . . . had carried out a long cherished scheme, now at last made practicable by her increasing reputation and income as a writer. Taking a woman friend with her as companion and secretary, she had left England, and travelled slowly about Europe, staying now here, now there, as fancy dictated or a good background presented itself for a story. Financially the trip had been a success. She had gathered material for two full-length novels, the scenes laid respectively in Madrid and Carcassonne, and written a series of short stories dealing with detective adventures in Hitlerite Berlin, and also a number of travel articles; thus more than replenishing the treasury . . . As soon as she got back to London, she moved to a new flat in Mecklenburg Square, and settled down to work at the Carcassonne novel.

Gaudy Night

Chapter 17
Money—for a Taxi

Not too long after we had established a private practice, I remember remarking to my colleagues that if every woman who walked into our office had a disposable income of €30,000 per annum her options, like Harriet's, would increase exponentially. There is nothing like money for buying you choice. You can decide where you want to live and how much time you want to spend there. You are free to leave the matrimonial home and rent 'a room of one's own'. You can decide which part of the globe you wish to explore and who your travelling companion will be. You can return to college to continue your education. Even the legal ideal of freedom of speech descends from the heights to become a daily practice. When you are not afraid of the results of your words you acquire the freedom to share what you are thinking and feeling. Money buys a lot of things but it's the intangibles that we can purchase with it, like freedom of movement and voice and self-fulfillment, that are priceless.

Sayers makes it perfectly clear that she is of the same opinion, even at a time when independent means would have been available to relatively few women. Harriet, with her own money, even enough to support a travelling companion, is free to come and go as she pleases before returning to her new home in London. When she moves into her flat she can begin to write and look forward again to publishing her ideas. Sayers has endowed Harriet with money and thus with three attributes that the author prizes: an education on which to base her self-employment, freedom of movement and a voice.

This is, of course, the privilege of wealth. Wealth is a relative condition and not easy to capture or define. Think of a woman in an unhappy marriage. If she has been used to a great deal of money there is little appetite for living on half or a quarter of what has brought her comfort. If she has been used to very little the question becomes how much money is enough to go it alone? How much do I need to feel secure? After all, rich or poor, you have put a great deal of time and effort, physical and emotional, into this marriage. You are not inclined to let it go easily. Even if you are being physically or verbally abused.

It is often the wealthy who find it more difficult to move than those who are barely getting by on their overdraft, or even their social welfare cheques. Sometimes women in possession of a substantial income will not find the courage to leave a destructive relationship while others will move with their children to the shelters. The reasons for staying or going are many and all the more compelling by being interwoven. 'He is a very good father and they love him': how do you bear the responsibility for rehousing and reshaping the lives of everyone else in the family? Will they decide that they come from a 'broken' home or a 'better' one? Even if 'better' will they have less opportunity and comfort in life without a father, and his wealth? Older children can participate in discussions about where they want to live and with whom but for young children the decisions must be made for them. When you feel well and truly stuck, wedged into the demands of your life, demands that feel both defining and trifling, all the money in the world will not help you to pry yourself loose. For reasons that are legion, many people, rich and poor, both mothers and fathers, choose to stay together 'for the sake of the children'.

Like a lot of things in life, money is, in the end, neither the problem nor the solution. Money helps and money hinders: too little will not always inhibit you and too much just might. Yet, without doubt, most of us would rather have more of it than less. It does buy us options, room to manoeuvre, the real possibility to reshape our lives. Sometimes all we want is security, just enough money to get home in a taxi.

In the developed world there are now many women with that personal income of €30,000 and some with a great deal more. This is an advance that can be directly attributed to education and anti-discrimination legislation. In the United States, for example, girls have always out-performed the boys at school. Now they are doing so in greater numbers and at higher levels. Women have formed the majority of college graduates since 1980. For over thirty years. Which leads us to the conclusion that some wives are now better educated than their husbands and many of these women have become the main family breadwinner. But it is still only some. Most wives, as we have seen, do not earn more than their husbands.

What are the implications of even some women being better educated than their husbands and earning substantial incomes of their own? Claudia Goldin, a professor of economics at Harvard, tells us that 'more educated women are healthier, live longer, have healthier children, more stable marriages and higher incomes.'[1] More stable marriages? She has enough money to leave. If she stays, she certainly has more bargaining power within the home, but does this power lead to stability or undermine it? Why would we assume that when it is a wife who earns more than her husband that the marriage will be more egalitarian. Why wouldn't she become as domineering as he used to be? She who pays the piper calls the tune, doesn't she?

Perhaps this is one of the reasons that everywhere in the developed world marriage is on the decline. Women will no longer tolerate a subservient role in relationships and now they do not have to. Divorce rates continue to rise and those who do marry are delaying the date. Both women and men are choosing in ever increasing numbers to cohabit, often serially. Self-supporting women now no longer need to marry up, to be taken care of, to be protected. Today they want a relationship based not on money—they have that already—but on partnership. They want intimacy, respect and definitely a more equal division of household labour and parenting duties. If men do not want these kinds of partnerships, and it seems that perhaps they do not, then there will be fewer and fewer marriages.

As Sayers said, it is no longer a case of any husband is better than none at all.

The history of feminism has shown us how women have been eager to enter the man's world of paid work. If marriage, albeit as a profoundly revised institution, is to survive as one of the foundational institutions of our culture, men are going to have to be just as enthusiastic about entering the world of women's unpaid work. A very interesting question has been posed by Janet Reibstein in light

---

1. Goldin, Claudia. 'Alpha Wives: The Trend and the Truth', in *The New York Times*, 24 January 2010.

of this decline of marriage. A psychologist at the University of Exeter, she wonders can we make the next cultural shift demanded by the effects of feminism. Her question is, can we now value in men what we have always valued in women? Or, I would suggest, a related but equally important question: can men now value in men what they purport to value in women? How do we all feel about the new gentleman?

Although gender role stereotypes are deeply embedded in our psyches we cannot return to the *status quo ante* feminism. We have to find new ways to share and care for each other because we have no choice—women are not going back.

Furthermore, I would not be without hope that men will join the revolution sooner rather than later.[2] In the first instance they are very relieved to be sharing the financial responsibility. But, secondly, whatever they actually still do, a growing proportion of younger men are beginning to realise that they want what women have. She enjoys the positive feedback earned by being a good parent, from running a well-regulated home and from her job. He is getting his sense of self-worth almost entirely from his job. Younger men are repeatedly saying that they want to balance moneymaking and caretaking. They want a life and they look for it in an egalitarian relationship. Sayers herself suggests that right relationship is a matter of 'very delicate balance'. She has her character, Miss de Vine say to Harriet, that being with a man who considers the woman in his life his equal means that, 'You needn't be afraid of losing your independence; he will always force it back on you. If you ever find any kind of repose with him, it can only be the repose of very delicate balance.'[3]

Wanting and acquiring are two different things. It is not the ideals of the young that are the problem, it is the structures within which they are forced to operate. Which leads us to quite a catch-22: the young want to change, if they do then when they grow up they will be in charge and can change the structures. But how can they really change when the inhibiting structures remain in place? We have seen that there is not enough parental leave or creche facilities, employers demand hours that are not family friendly. Both men and women are

---

2. For a full discussion of the 'Gender Dilemma' see my *Care, Justice and Gender: A New Harmony for Family Values* (Dublin: Veritas, 2009).
3. *Gaudy Night*, 546

punished for attending to their offspring, albeit in different ways and for different reasons. When are we going to get enough wise men at the top to pass laws that will ensure family-friendly work practices? But why would they want such laws that will ruin their profit margins?

These young people know what the workplace has not yet grasped, that there will be no really happy families without gender equality. She is not going back to a state of uncritical admiration and he knows it. She definitely wants it all but she no longer has any intention of trying to do it all alone. Or, to put it another way, if you live alone you do not mind doing all the housework, but if you live with someone else the unfairness of that arrangement becomes intolerable.

Clearly, individual decisions are not easy to make even when there is money in the bank. How much more difficult is it to create a life for yourself out of virtually nothing at all? The United Nations Development Fund for Women (UNIFEM) estimates (exact figures are hard to come by in the developing world) that women worldwide account for two thirds of all working hours and produce half the food, but earn just ten percent of the world's income and own less than one percent of the world's property. They believe that as many as seventy percent of the world's poor are women. This situation is not going to improve any time soon as UNIFEM also notes that financing for dedicated gender-quality projects represented less than five percent of total funds provided by the Organisation for Economic and Co-operation Development (OECD) in 2006. Gender has been noted but it is hardly a priority.

Despite the almost incredible obstacles, the multitudes attempting the daily struggle of trying to survive on $1 a day, the malnutrition and early deaths of those who fail, there are green shoots. These tiny signs of life and hope are called micro-loans, an appropriately labeled form of finance as the loans range from US$50 to $500. In Haiti, for example the NGO, Moun Pou Moun (Person by Person) currently has twenty women repaying such loans with which they started their own small businesses. The availability of the loan, coupled with a fair interest rate, means that these women can now support their families. In Kenya, a group of women growing fresh flowers for shipment to the United Kingdom were able to secure higher wages and better working conditions by pressuring buyers with the aid of London based 'fair-trade' activists. In these two small examples, from Haiti to

Africa, we see women earning more than their husbands and being the primary, or only, bread winners.

One of Sayers' minor characters and a friend of Harriet's is Eilund Price who confides to Wimsey that she only lends money to women because 'they pay back'.[4] Price sounds like a director of the World Bank. This Bank estimates that almost thirty percent of employment in the developing world is generated by the informal economy. They like to lend to women as they estimate that women reinvest ninety percent of their income in their families and communities, compared with men who reinvest only thirty to forty percent in their families. In agreement with the World Bank, the Grameen Bank[5] reports, in words that echo Sayers, that women are much more likely to repay their loans than men.

One of the foundational principles of small financial groups like Moun Pou Moun, and of global giants like the World Bank, is self-sustainability. This, of course, is a condition that Sayers thinks is so important that she gifted it to her heroine, Harriet. It is what feminism would like to gift to every woman, and every man.

UNIFEM has argued that it is extremely important to introduce *concrete targets* and *goals* into *reform plans* to improve the situation of girls and women worldwide. This, they say, would help *policy makers* and *civil society groups* design *programs that are more responsive to gender concerns*. The italics are mine, to emphasise that for rich women in the developed world and for poor women in the developing world the plan to achieve financial independence and self-sustainability consists of the same elements even as we acknowledge that the needs of one group are far greater. It is the existence of UNIFEM itself that is witness to the fact that women are still, not yet, equal citizens of the world.

---

4. *Strong Poison*, 103
5. http://www.grameen-info.org This bank was started in Chittigong, India, to provide loans to the rural poor.

'. . . in my opinion . . . the ladies were most adorable when they adorned and inspired and did not take any active part in affairs.'

Strong Poison

Chapter 18
Women and Politics: A Political Agenda

To start this chapter, I must first read the papers online to see what they are saying about women and politics. Perhaps not too coincidentally my eyes are drawn to a headline in the Toronto Sun: 'We need more of the fairer sex in politics'. The fairer sex is just one more epithet that is all part and parcel of the adorable and adorning ones. Politics is something about which they shouldn't bother their silly little heads. But this time the writer is making the incongruous suggestion, still far from fulfilled, that the ladies should take an 'active part in affairs'.

As of late 2011, in the developed and enlightened world, women are not well represented in their parliaments. Women hold less than seventeen percent of seats in the United States Congress. In Australia approximately twenty-five percent of the seats in their lower house are held by women, while in the United Kingdom the number falls to twenty-two percent. The Nordic countries come closer to equal representation with numbers that range between approximately forty to forty-five percent.[1] Because women have occupied these positions for decades one might expect that their numbers would be steadily growing. They are not; in fact, if anything, they are declining. Only in two countries, Rwanda and Andorra, do women share half of parliamentary representation, their numbers being fifty-six percent and fifty percent respectively. While we note these two exceptions, and acknowledge that the progress made by women in the Nordic countries is well documented, we still must ask what is wrong with the rest of the world? And why is our parliamentary progress so slow?

---

1. 'Women in National Parliaments'. www.ipu.org/wmn

Women have been occupying seats in the British House of Commons since long before Sayers introduced us to Peter and Harriet. The Countess Markievicz, of Anglo Irish descent but married to a Polish Count, stood for election to a Dublin constituency in 1918 while she was in Holloway prison in England. She found herself there as a direct result of her political beliefs and activities: she was a member of Sinn Fein and had taken part in the Easter Uprising of 1916. She was duly elected but, to protest the foreign occupation, she refused to take her seat. Nancy, Viscountess Astor, was the first women to occupy her seat in the House of Commons which she did in 1919 and she held it until her retirement in 1945. We could argue that these two women were exceptional, one for depth of her political convictions, the other for her bank balance. But, it is surely not a coincidence that both of them were elected contemporaneously with the passing of the Representation of the People Act, 1918, which gave women the limited right to vote—if they were over the age of thirty, and if they were a landowner or married to one. This was only the first step in almost half a century of vilification, of real suffering and imprisonment which preceded the achievement of universal suffrage in Britain for all adults over twenty-one years of age in1928.

Even before Sayers began writing, there were women like these who were engaged in formal and public political life, taking their place with men in parliamentary chambers, right at the heart of government. But the conundrum remains: For nearly a century, all across the developed world, women have been in a position to vote women into power. Today, if women do not like the way the world is working they have it within their grasp to do something very real about changing it. Why are there still so few women politicians?

We might posit, as many have done, that politics is a profession that is too hard for women, too physically demanding. Certainly, there are many traditionally male jobs, like fire fighting, where women have made little impact, perhaps because it is an occupation that often requires a great deal of physical strength. Campaigning is tough but so is agricultural labour, standing at a factory bench, even housework; yet women have traditionally hoed, planted, weeded and harvested. With babies on their backs. Women have no trouble shaking hands and we know they are good at holding babies for photos ops so what else could be holding them back from entering the political arena?

For those who did make the attempt, other obstacles were put in their path. There were—and are—a lot of men like Sayers' law clerk who felt sure Wimsey would agree with him that 'the ladies were most adorable when they adorned or inspired but did not take any part in public affairs'. These men formed networks of support for other men. The Old Boys Club, across whichever sea you liked to mention, did not support female candidates with public praise, private support or, most importantly, money. They invited them to share their beds but not their responsibility for public life. There was also the enemy within, the problem of begrudging women. Women did not, for a long time, trust or admire other women. They chose male surgeons and architects and preferred male chefs and hairdressers. There was a general consensus amongst both men and women that women did not really belong in politics, or indeed in any other public role other than nursing and teaching.

By and large, women have recovered their wits and now acknowledge freely, even with joy, that women can be the best of surgeons. Men, however, are still having trouble admitting women to positions of power and prestige, even when the women are surgeons. Nonetheless, it seems fair to say that the feminist movement has so altered the general perception of women and their abilities that many female leaders have emerged. We are familiar with names like Golda Meir, Margaret Thatcher, Benazir Bhutto, Helen Clark and today, Angela Merkel and Julia Gillard. In fact, since 1945, the year that saw the end of the war in which women played such a significant part, there have been fifty-three women Prime Ministers, although, admittedly, thirty-four of them have held this position for less than a year and others for less than two years. The percentage of women prime ministers at any one time around the world is tiny. They are, by any standard, exceptional women.

Whilst it has been possible to sometimes elect female leaders, women are still struggling to achieve equal representation within existing political parties. Nonetheless, due to decades of concerted and persistent agitation there is a growing world-wide consensus amongst male political leaders that there should be more women in parliament. Governments themselves and the individual parties within them have both taken action. In more than fifty countries, members of existing political parties who believe that they should have an equal number of women within their ranks have amended their internal party rules accordingly.[2] At last count approximately forty governments have introduced gender quotas in elections for their national parliaments to achieve this end, even if the requirement is only for twenty percent or thirty percent or forty percent. Perhaps a more interesting way to present the quota would be to say there is to be 'no more than sixty percent of either sex'. If looked at from this gender-neutral perspective men would be forced to experience how it felt to be offered a quota of as little as twenty per cent of any legislative chamber. Whatever the figure, this kind of global movement by male dominated governments and political parties must be seen as some degree of success for feminist persistence.

Apart from being unpopular in many quarters, or, indeed, perhaps because they are unpopular, the question of quotas is a complex one. For example, there are many levels at which the quota system can be inserted into the electoral or party process, from the original pool of candidates, to how many must stand for election, to how many must actually be elected. All operate with varying effects, while sometimes the legal mandate to impose quotas is even ignored and the non-compliance is not punished. Even when quotas are imposed the strategy does not always succeed. For example, in the United Kingdom, where the aim of quotas is to enlarge the pool of candidates willing to stand for election we have already noted that only twenty-two percent of women are members of parliament.

The same unpredictable result can occur when we compare countries where no quotas are imposed, as is the case, for example, in the United States and New Zealand. The latter, with thirty-two percent of women in the lower house, manages to nearly double the rate achieved in the former. It may be that there is a more favourable attitude towards women in New Zealand—it was after all, the first country to give women the vote in 1893 and Helen Clark was witness to the efficacy of a woman as prime minister of this nation for eight years. On the other hand, the price, the actual dollars required, to enter a Congressional race may be too high for most women in America where, as elsewhere, women do not have the same economic power as men. Both a change in attitude and a limit on how much money

---

2. Quota Project: Global Database of Quotas for Women .http://www.quotaproject. org

can be spent on an election campaign are necessary for women to advance in numbers as legislators.

Should women support any and every woman willing to stand for election simply because she is a woman? I think the answer to this question at this moment in history is a simple 'yes'. Despite the fact that my own research tells me that many men and women will disagree with me. The more popular view is that we should vote for the most qualified candidate irrespective of their sex. For myself, I find it hard to forget that in the primary contests of 2008, African Americans voted between seventy and ninety percent for Barack Obama while Hilary Clinton managed to attract a bare majority of female voters. Until women are equal in every other walk of life, women need to vote for women. I would argue, in line with critical mass theory, that women are unlikely to have an impact until their numbers grow from a few token individuals into a substantial minority of all legislators. This, of course, depends on elected women being of like mind and working towards the same ends.

Would women bring to a legislature anything that was different? There is evidence that women, even when they enjoy no critical mass whatsoever, focus on gender issues. Overall, they have a vision of society in which burdens and benefits are shared equally by all. More specifically, their objectives tend to fall under the headings of solidarity and care for the poor. They support children and the elderly, perhaps because they are who women take care of even when they are working outside the home. The earliest, lone female members of the British parliament are cases in point. Countess Markievicz was concerned with solidarity and a vision of equality for all citizens. Nancy Astor focused upon women and children, temperance (which would relieve women and children of the behaviour of drunken men), education and nursery schools. Ellen Wilkinson, who fought for women's suffrage as a member of the Communist Party, was elected for the Labour Party in 1924. Her concern for the poor and solidarity with the unemployed caused her to lead a march of 200 unemployed workers to London. She was also responsible for the introduction of free milk for school children.

Across the Atlantic, every state had given women the right to vote by 1920 but again not without a great deal of suffering. Jeannette Pickering Rankin, became the first woman to sit in Congress. She was a lifelong pacifist, a founding member of the Women's International League for Peace and Freedom, and was the only member of Congress to vote against both world wars. She campaigned against the Korean war and the Vietnam war, leading a protest demonstration of thousands of women in Washington, DC. She was also an ardent suffragist who agreed with Jane Adams that slum conditions were worsened by women's inability to vote. She introduced legislation to provide for health clinics, midwife education, and visiting nurse programs in an effort to reduce the infant mortality rate. When she died at the age of ninety-two she bequeathed her property to help 'mature, unemployed women workers'.

Suppressed minorities are always at a structural disadvantage, be they black students seeking an education after the Civil Rights movement in the United States, the women of Saudi Arabia who will, they say, be allowed to vote in local elections in 2015 or even the relatively privileged female employees of European corporations. To assist these people to rise to equal civil and moral status, not only are properly administered quotas essential but the members of the suppressed group, like the Gdansk dock workers of Poland in the 1980s that became a trade union for a third of workers, must work in solidarity with each other.

Not all women will fight against the entrenched power of patriarchy, or are even aware of their own assimilation into the system. Margaret Thatcher was one such and yet, I would have voted for her. Looking within the system, I am also in favour of the more nuanced suggestion that argues that what we really need are 'critical actors'. These are politicians, both male and female, who will individually or collectively, work to bring about legislation that is woman and minority friendly. The political path to equality therefore looks like this: quotas to achieve critical mass and critical mass to bolster the work of critical actors.

'The entrenched power of patriarchy' seems to many a dated phrase. You would drown in groans of oh-my-god-not-that-again if you used it. By relentlessly pointing to the lack of equality in our society, feminists are accused of nagging as they try to talk their way towards equality. They lay out the problem, they explain, they highlight the injustices, they raise their voices, they lower their voices, they speak in tongues. To no avail. Those with the power pretend to be listening but all they do is ask to have the problem explained again, to make the powerless keep repeating the problem, over and over and over again. For over fifty years. It is a very effective tactic. Tell me again, what is it that you women want?

There have been improvements. Constant talking about violence against women has turned private drunken attacks into the crimes of assault and battery and rape. Constant 'nagging' about the same old topics of welfare issues, women and children's health, maternity and paternity leave, education and care of the elderly, equal pay, is gradually eroding resistance. The result is that it is acknowledged everywhere that gender matters in politics, a fact that had been denied by men in power for a long time. Men were used to seeing themselves as genderless humans. But, if gender really matters then male politicians will have to start seeing themselves as male humans no matter how degrading they find it to no longer personify the sole and exclusive definition of what it is to be a human being.

I think it would be a good idea if all governments followed one Swedish initiative which arranged for a series of gender seminars to be attended by all politicians, senior civil servants, church leaders and university presidents as well as heads of government sponsored TV and radio. At least then we would all know that they know what it is that women want. If we could finally put an end to that question then they could be judged on whether, or to what extent, they had given it to us. It is possible that such a learning experience might generate a greater number of critical actors, in and out of politics, who would agree with a redrafted headline for the Toronto Sun which would read, 'Politics needs more of the sex that seeks fairness'.

Bess of Hardwick's daughter had been a great intellectual, indeed, but something of a holy terror; uncontrollable by her menfolk, undaunted by the Tower, contemptuously silent before the Privy Council, an obstinate recusant, a staunch friend and implacable enemy and a lady with a turn for invective remarkable even in an age when few mouths suffered from mealiness. She seemed in fact, to be the epitome of every alarming quality which a learned woman is popularly credited with developing.

Gaudy Night

Chapter 19
Feminism: It's the Housework, Stupid

We are all equal now, the women's movement is part of history, finding its origin and fulfillment in a previous generation. This is the story of the backlash, of anti-feminism and we hear it all the time.

It is a story that makes women, especially the young ones, frightened to appear out of date and old fashioned. So, they stop speaking about their experience, about the truth of their daily lives, because the truth is another story entirely.

The truth is everything that I have laid out in the preceding chapters of this book. The truth is that women across the developed world earn from ten to twenty percent less than men even when men's longer working hours are taken into account. The truth is that women, whether seeking promotion from the shop floor or to the ranks of senior partner in a law firm will hide the fact that they are pregnant until the promotion comes through. Their men folk will rely on the same pregnancy to actively seek promotion on the proud grounds that he has another mouth to feed. That little mouth is, of course, a metaphorical one because he will never step off his career path to parent for the same amount of time as she does. The double-standard, along with the double message, is still alive and well.

We are told that we live in the halcyon era of post-feminism. The myth that we are in the age of post-feminism relies, paradoxically, upon the idea that feminism has been taken into account. That is to say, the feminist movement, with its network of related concerns, has done its work, the task is completed, the goal achieved. Even when we know, are presented with evidence every day, despite decades of consciousness raising and legislation, that sexism, racism, classism and homophobia persist. Because we know this does not in any way approach the truth it must be said that the notion of post feminism be named for what it is: anti-feminism.

This is the kind of double-bind that could drive you mad: women are equal but not equal. How do we explain these two completely contradictory propositions, one an aspiration, the other a reality?

I think they are best explained by a close examination of the established hierarchies of power and gender. Men hold the power, the purse strings and the political institutions and they are not going to relax their grip anytime soon. The aim of feminism has always been to undermine the established hierarchies of power and gender to the mutual benefit of both sexes; so that each sex can care and be taken care of by turn. But this project has failed, or has at least not been fully realised.

This close examination, this peeling off of the layers of politically correct non-sense, will expose the reality of women's lives in the public and the private spheres over the past half century.

Before the movement that we know as second wave feminism began to roll in the 1960s women and men lived by what we can call the The Old Sexual Contract. It was well established territory and everyone knew their roles and the rules by which they were to play. He will function in the public sphere and be the primary breadwinner. She will work, unpaid, and be dependent on her man, in the private sphere as the parent and home maker. Men had the power and women were subordinate. Admittedly, this is a bald description, without nuance, but nonetheless it does express the very essence of the old established hierarchy of power and gender.

This contract depended very largely on the belief that gender roles are innate. This is a belief that is as reassuring as it is dangerous because it precludes any questioning of the *status quo*. It asserts that the way things are is the way they are meant to be. Women can stay home with their babies and men can go out to work and these cultural requirements are justified because they are based upon immutable nature. Life might not have been comfortable but it was settled—until some feminist philosophers proposed another view, one that showed how gender roles were, in fact, social constructions. As de Beauvoir put it, women are made not born.

So, if gender roles are not innate, some women will say, after the birth of the baby, I want to get back to work, and he might say, I want to stay home and be a house husband. Well, do it. Feminism has made that much possible. In the real world, however, we know that there are not too many couples like them. The number of men who want to rock the cradle is so small that they will not rock the gender system at all. The most usual scenario is for her to work both in and out of the home and for him to work only out of the home as before. Some women give up employment for years, saying, I couldn't leave the baby, s/he is so wonderful, s/he will grow up so quickly, this time is so precious. This woman takes her education and takes her talents and pops them under a stone and is very comfortable with her opinion of herself and society's opinion of her. Everyone knows she is being a good woman in choosing not just the fact of motherhood but the unreconstructed role of motherhood. Others will try to do both jobs, to be 'super mum' but will find that they are not succeeding as they would wish at either job and so return to the home full time. While she is struggling with the so-called 'work-life balance', he does not have to say a word. In fact, if he is subsequently asked for an opinion, he will say, 'we decided that she would stay home, we both wanted one of us with the baby rather than a nanny.'

'We' decided? This outcome is really much bigger than both of them. The cultural expectations are so deeply ingrained that it is very hard for a woman to leave her baby and for a man to stay home. These expectations played a very large part in what they believe they so freely decided. If men wanted even just one year of parental leave do you really think for a moment that we would not have legislated for it decades ago? They make banking regulations and break them at will. They have trade unions and they pay as little as they can. They have health and safety programs for work sites and build as quickly and cheaply as possible, whatever the risk. They pass laws against prostitution and use trafficked women by the thousands at the World Cup soccer tournament or the Super Bowl. It is incredible to think that men could not arrange to pass legislation that would give them the deepest desire of their hearts: a year at home with their new born.

But, you contest, what if he was self-employed? What would become of his business, his factory, his legal practice or pharmacy? Nothing really. He is not irreplaceable, his business partners would fill in for him, the second in charge would run the factory, a locum or junior partner would run his law firm or pharmacy. If he can plan a moon shot, he could plan for his replacement. He wouldn't make as much money, the competition might make up some of the distance he had put between them and himself but he is on the 'daddy-track' and that is what happens when you put your children before your job. If he thinks that is such an appalling outcome how is it that it has been all right for her to accept it?

A young male doctor described a female colleague as a ball-breaker. We were at my daughter's birthday dinner so I raised my eyebrows, just to let him know I didn't approve but that I wasn't going to make a scene. Only in jest, he said. Right, of course it was. She must have been pretty good at her job to provoke this response. Yet, I wonder how many of his male colleagues he refers to as cunt-crusher? None probably because I just thought up the term when I realised that there was no derogatory equivalent for men. That 'only in jest' response is a killer. It means, 'where's your sense of humour?' and it is very hard to be told all the time that you have no sense of humour, that we were all just having a good time together until you, you kill-joy, came along to ruin the party. It does tend to shut women up (see above for the silence of my raised eyebrows), to silence their critical and analytical voice, to take away their power, to return them to the box labeled 'passive gender'. To make them the victims of sexual harassment. To point out one more time that men are treating women as sexual objects is not popular conversation at the dinner table.

Part of the backlash is generated by the realisation that the political is the personal. If you change too many laws you will initiate too many changes in our personal lives. Men might have to reassess their relationship to their work and their wives. It seems that the Old Sexual Contract is not so old, it still thrives and is very familiar.

What then is the basis of the New Sexual Contract, the one that insists that women and men are now equal? That one that is predicated upon the assertion that we no longer have need for any feminist politics because the goal is achieved.

This new sexual contract operates largely within the public sphere and this time it is made between women and the state. Due to the early agitations of the feminist movement women are now well educated, working women. With learning and money they understand themselves to be independent individuals with freedom and choice. These women can now pursue their own personal desires.

From Gucci shoes and Mulberry handbags at the top end to holidays in the Mediterranean a little further down the salary scale, they are full participants in the consumer culture of global capitalism. They have their own cars and buy their own homes. With readily available contraception they can have sex like men.

The state too is delighted with its self-image, the proponent of diversity, tolerance and equality. It knows itself to be 'gender aware', thoroughly enlightened and modern, looking down on those nations that do not treat their women so well. It peddles a pro-family, conservative form of feminism as part of this new sexual contract. The best of states provide paid leave to allow workers to care for elderly family members even though it knows that it will be women who will take up these offers. But the state has done its part; the individual is responsible for their own, personal choices.

We know that women are not yet equal so what has happened here? What has happened is that the doors have opened and the old system has accommodated itself just enough to allow a form of liberal feminism to walk into the halls of power. Women have been assimilated into the old system but the radical challenge for a new social order that was the real promise of feminism has been subverted.

Women today are in double trouble. How exactly are they to behave inside the male system of power and hierarchy now that they have arrived? How should they appear and act as they find themselves in competition with men on a daily basis? They have to be both feminine and masculine. She has to be a desirable female in a male dominated system. She cannot be too powerful for fear that this will detract from her desireability. If she is not attractive enough a successful woman might be seen as a feminist (or a ball breaker) so she will weigh herself down with expensive equipment. Ruinous stiletto heels; no healthy, flat and comfortable shoes. But how she dresses for work is, of course, a personal choice.

Just like her sex life. She now must define sex as men always did, as light-hearted sport, as recreational pleasure because she is liberated and modern. But she can only really have sexual relations with a man on his terms, in a way that pleases him. She cannot say no to sex indefinitely without being seen as frigid or weird. She can certainly pay half the restaurant bill but she cannot ask him out or propose marriage to him. She cannot be too like him because this would mean she was exercising power and control which is still his prerogative. He is still in charge of the parameters and pace of the relationship. Feminism has not altered the fact that a woman must get a man and a man must be successful, preferably with money. But how and when she has sex is, of course, a personal choice.

When she returns to work after having children she has once again left feminist politics behind her and returned to the art of compromise. We can recall that Carol Gilligan described this as giving up on relationship for the sake of relationships. In practice this means that she no longer attempts to negotiate an end to the inequality of housework and child care but endlessly casts around for ways to manage these dual responsibilities. Note carefully, there is no challenge here to the Old Sexual Contract. But, of course, this is all a matter of personal choice.

When she returns to work she seeks compromise with her employer. She looks for flexible working hours or part-time employment to achieve that work-life balance. Her husband gets on with his job without complaint from her and without reducing his hours. He is a prime favourite with his employer. Her need to compromise means that she is condemned, more or less, to subordinate wage-earning capacity for the term of her natural life. But, of course, this is all a matter of personal choice.

What is clear is that we now have two sexual contracts operating in tandem. You could be excused for thinking you were suffering from double vision, listening to double messages operating a double standard. The new contract is the old contract with sugar coating. Governments, like the member states of the European Union, or international organisations like the United Nations, talk about 'Gender Mainstreaming' but this is a liberal term that lacks radical intent. We are back to the days of liberal feminism, where women are assimilated into the structures of gender and power that remain in existence.

Radical feminism is still abhorred even when it is clear that its goal is a degree of social criticism that aims to achieve equality for all in a world where patriarchy has not given up one iota of its power.

Granted, we now have huge numbers of very well educated women who are in receipt of very good salaries. But this educated and independently earning self is an individual. She is cut off from her sisters and is largely unaware of any feminist politics. She is unaware that it is feminist politics to which she owes her current happy state. She is unaware that she is still needed to be part of a feminist movement that will make a continuous and intense analysis of the oppression of the group to which she belongs and especially on behalf of those who are not white and who are poor. This new, government led sexual contract looks like a serious, well intentioned, real response to serious, well intentioned, real feminism but in fact and in effect it is subversive. What appears on the surface to be supportive of feminism radically undermines the project.

What the world really needs now is for more of our educated, earning young women to be more like Mary Cavendish (1556–1632), wife to Gilbert Talbot, the 7th Earl of Shrewsbuy, but known to Sayers as the daughter of Bess of Hardwick. Which is to say that we want today's young women to be "the epitome of every alarming quality which a learned woman is popularly credited with developing". Maybe then we can re-activate the struggle to achieve the power and the promise of true feminism.

Wimsey considered for a moment.

'Were you friends?'

'No'. The word broke out with a kind of repressed savagery that startled him. 'Philip wasn't the sort of man to make a friend of a woman. He wanted devotion. I gave him that . . . But I couldn't stand being made a fool of. I couldn't stand being put on probation like an office-boy, to see if I was good enough to be condescended to. I quite thought he was honest when he said he didn't believe in marriage—and then it turned out that it was a test, to see whether my devotion was abject enough. Well, it wasn't. I didn't like having matrimony offered as a bad-conduct prize.'

'I don't blame you,' said Wimsey . . .

'Yes—it's ridiculous—but humiliating too. Well, there it is. I thought Philip had made both himself and me ridiculous, and the minute I saw that—well, the whole thing simply shut down—flop!'

She sketched a gesture of finality.

'I quite see that,' said Wimsey. 'Such a Victorian attitude, too, for a man with advanced ideas. He for God only, she for God in him, and so on.'

Strong Poison

Chapter 20
Friendship

Given the enduring popularity of marriage it is odd to discover that even today deep friendships between women and men are rare.

Certainly, at the time that Harriet Vane and Peter Wimsey were testing the possibilities of their relationship, women and men inhabited different worlds. Their conversations take place between the two Great Wars, in an England that is only slowly beginning to acknowledge that women, though inhabitants of the same society, and the ones who preside over the moral nursery of their offspring, are rational beings. Although women had been paying taxes for centuries they had just been granted the right to vote and, happily for Harriet in her current predicament, were now considered to be citizens who could be trusted with the responsibility of jury duty.

As this particular conversation takes place, Harriet and Peter are also inhabiting zones with very different comfort levels due to their personal circumstances. Harriet is in prison, awaiting trial, charged with poisoning her lover, a crime for which she will hang if found guilty. Wimsey has taken it upon himself to prove her innocence. At his disposal are not only a keen intelligence and substantial wealth but also all the privileges that a rigid class system has to offer the brother of a Duke. At Wimsey's end of the social scale they still dress for dinner, assisted by those at the other end of the scale, those in service: the manservant or maid who are as commonplace as their fellow servants who cook and serve that dinner. This is the world of Upstairs/Downstairs and Downton Abbey, the unquestioned, natural order where the labouring classes serve the wealthy. It was a world, the heart of an empire, of radical separations where the gap between social and economic classes and between races was as wide as it was between men and women. Classism, racism and sexism were all alive and well. For white, western couples, the public sphere of power and politics was reserved for men with money and the private one of domesticity was the domain of women, whatever their level of income. Even for those in service, men still had the edge: the butler was more important than the housekeeper. These arrangements were kept in place by all the forces that State and Church could muster. An arrangement perfectly captured by Wimsey's reference to Milton where the poet describes the beauty of Adam and Eve: she the image of subjection and gentleness, and Adam, formed strong to have absolute rule: 'He for God only, she for God in him.'[1]

But that way of viewing the world is supposed to be old-fashioned, behind us now. Whatever our economic class, we are not 'spouses' anymore, we are 'partners'. The emphasis has shifted from the constrictions of the 'marriage contract' to the freedom and possibilities of a 'relationship'.

This relationship between equals is to be rooted in love, companionship and sexual pleasure, all of which is to add up to mutually satisfying intimacy. There is more than an emphasis on the concept of mutuality, it is the rationale for the entire enterprise. Mutuality implies that the partners hold each other in equal respect, where the sharing and caring that happens in the relationship is not lop-sided but reciprocal. This is the bliss of equality, the consummation devoutly to be wished, what we proclaim proudly and vigorously, what we claim is the entitlement of every man and every woman. Today, if a man mistreats a woman or misbehaves, her mother and father both will tell her to leave him and then help her to do it. We have even, finally, passed laws prohibiting rape within marriage. Once upon a time, in what we like to call the good old days, she would have been told to ignore it, or turn a blind eye; she had made her bed, she must lie on it. Today, with the goal of mutual respect in both word and action it would be easy to assume that husbands and wives are friends. The fact is that sometimes they are but far too often they are not.

When young people go to co-ed schools and to university they make friends with the opposite sex. If three or four of these friends subsequently move into a house together the girls are not expected to

---

1.   Milton, *Paradise Lost*, Book 4, 288–324.

do all the cooking for the boys or to wash their underwear. The boys are not expected to change the oil in the girls' cars or to take out their garbage. They are friends but they are independent; they do not have expectations of being cared for by any of their flat-mates. A flat-mate or a room-mate is not the same thing at all as a mate. (Unless, of course, you are an Australian and then mate and friend are one and the same).

It is this question of expectations that is at the heart of the problem. We all have expectations of each other which are generated and determined by the nature of our relationship. The boss expects you to be at work on time. This expectation arises out of the culture and the institution that is the world of paid work. Once you are a couple then She is expected to do most of the cooking and the laundry and He is expected to take out the garbage and change the oil in the car. These expectations arise out of the culture and institution that is marriage. You can fuss and fume or compromise and negotiate all you want but the expectations are always there. And they deepen when children arrive.

It seems pretty clear that a boy and a girl can remain friends so long as they don't fall in love!

You would think that if people fell in love they would become even better friends. Not so; if they fall in love, they have to be very, very careful. Talk of engagements, marriage and permanence begins to subtly, but fundamentally, alter the relationship.

Once you take friendship and place it within the boundaries of the institution of marriage it becomes prey to all sorts of expectations and tensions. For example, Jim is no longer just your friend, he has become a husband, your husband. He is expected by both of you to work hard and earn money. If he becomes over-committed to the fulfilment of this expectation he might be having lunches with business associates, drinks after work with colleagues, or golf games with future prospects. He might be late getting home. Even if he phones it might be to tell you that he is going to be late rather than to ask does that fit in with your plans. He often expects you to socialise with his friends but he is not so keen on going out with the girls.

The problem is that the articulated dream of love, and marriage, and living happily ever after, does not match the unspoken reality.

We have created a new language of equality but kept the old expectations and meanings intact: partner doesn't mean partner, it still means spouse. And spouse means 'husband' or 'wife' and those two words bring a load of baggage that has nothing to do with equality. We are paying lip-service to the caring and sharing involved in partnership but deep down, inside ourselves, we don't believe in equality and so we don't practice it. We still hold deep-seated beliefs about what it means to be a good man or a good woman. The change in state to a husband or a wife, a mother or a father results in these beliefs becoming incompatible with a mutual and reciprocal relationship. Put simply, being wife and mother still means being in charge of the home and the children, a facilitating environment for everyone, even if she is employed outside the home. She is the provider of a balanced diet, clean clothes and a birthday gift for her mother-in-law. Being husband and father still means being in charge of bringing home the money, but his domestic contributions, like changing light bulbs or taxing the car, only occur at widely spaced intervals.

Take the couple, with two small children, who both work outside the home. He will agree to 'babysit' their children on Saturday afternoon while she goes to the mall with her mother. But so often he feels able to lie on the couch and watch a football match and not move unless the house catches fire. The odds are much better than even, according to all the research, that she won't come home to a bathroom that has been cleaned, or carpets that have been vacuumed, or an evening meal prepared, or babies bottles or school lunches prepared for the week - all things that she would have done if he had spent the afternoon on the golf course or even taken the children to the park.

We hear a lot about the new man and how things have changed, but taking the kids to the park or whipping up a souffle for the Saturday night dinner guests is the fun part and it is not the same as scouring the shower recess and being responsible for a steady supply of toilet paper. In 2007, data from 17,636 people residing in twenty-eight countries revealed that, overall, men averaged 9.41 hours of housework per week and women 21.13 hours. In a liberal democracy like Britain, the British man came in tenth place, performing only thirty-five percent of chores. Not unexpectedly, this was well below the more egalitarian Scandinavian countries. But, and this is the piece that pertains to the dangers of marriage for women, it was these same

Scandinavian countries which had the highest cohabitation rates. This is in line with the major finding of the study, that cohabiting couples are far more likely than those who are married to split housework. It is this key finding that indicates that it is the institution of marriage itself that changes the egalitarian nature of the relationship.[2] There appear to be well defined codes of behaviour for husbands and wives, particularly in relation to what we call 'women's work', that precludes the kind of sharing that many live-in lovers expect from each other.

This double-jobbing, where women can work outside the home if they choose but still remain almost entirely responsible for all the housework and parenting, is only the beginning. The friendship really begins to unravel when she can't complain about his 'babysitting' without getting a furious 'you're never satisfied' in response. We say out loud, unequivocally, that men and women are equal and therefore she has the right to complain. But this right is not enforceable. What good is the right to free speech if nobody listens? A right that is not enforceable is no right at all. Feminist theorists have consistently maintained that the ability to be able to insist on shared housework is the greatest indicator of equality in marriage. If he has greater power and more freedom to negotiate less domestic tasks and more recreation, can we really say that men and women come equally to marriage?

After too much of this, over years of it, she gives up on friendship. She doesn't ask any more, she learns not to nag, all for the sake of keeping the marriage intact. As Carol Gilligan puts it, she 'gives up on relationship for the sake of relationships'. She knows it is not easy for a single woman with children to prosper out there, either in the workplace or in social settings. She knows that the children love their dad and she doesn't want to deprive them of his company (even though the research tells us that fathers see more of their children after they are divorced than they did while living in the family home). Of course, she might, in the end, decide not to keep the marriage intact. She will then file for divorce and feminism will be blamed for the breakdown of the marriage and the ruin of the family.

---

2. Shannon Davis *et al*, 'Effects of Union Type on Division of Household Labor: Do Cohabiting Men Really Perform More Housework?', in the *Journal of Family Issues*, 8 (September 2007): 1246–1272.

With a friend, someone you consider your equal, someone you respect, you would want to do your fair share of everything. You pay attention to the needs of your friend so that one person is not continually having to ask the other for help, or being resentful that they are not getting it. You take responsibility so that you, yourself, will be worthy of respect. Then, when all the jobs are done, you can both take off your rubber gloves to relax and go and play together.

Harriet's previous relationship had been a failure in terms of friendship: Philip wasn't the sort of man to make a friend of a woman. He wanted devotion. But Wimsey is the sort of man to make a friend of a woman. He says,

> *As a matter of fact, I'd like somebody I could talk*
> *sensibly to, who would make life interesting. And I*
> *could give you lots of plots for your books.*

In effect, he is saying, we could collaborate. He goes on to insist that,

> *It would be great fun. So much more interesting than*
> *the ordinary kind (of woman/wife) who are only keen*
> *on clothes and people.*

He muses to himself:

> *She's got a sense of humour too—brains—one wouldn't*
> *be dull—one would wake up and there'd be a whole day*
> *for jolly things to happen in—and then one would come*
> *home and go to bed—and that would be jolly too—and*
> *while she was writing, I could go out and mess around,*
> *so we wouldn't either of us be dull.*

Are love and marriage dangerous for women? If entered into too soon, the answer is, yes.

The first thing you have to do is talk to your man about an equal split in housework and parenting. And the fact that first, you have to talk about it at all and second, you are definitely going to be the one who has to bring it up, tells you that there is still a problem for couples around the division of household labour. How many boys sit their girlfriends down for a serious chat, to make it clear to her that she is going to have to do her fair share of the housework and childminding?

But, if he is your friend this will be an easy conversation. If it turns out not to be an easy conversation then you have to pause and consider: He might be your sexual partner, he might even be your lover, but is he really your friend? We have already discovered again that actions speak louder than words so the better course is to live together for several years before you marry. Get into the habit of cohabiting equally. You need to be very sure, as Sayers warned so many decades ago, that you have a real friend with whom to share your life rather than with someone who wants you to be devoted to his needs.

Lightning Source UK Ltd.
Milton Keynes UK
UKOW02n1521280217

295538UK00001B/10/P